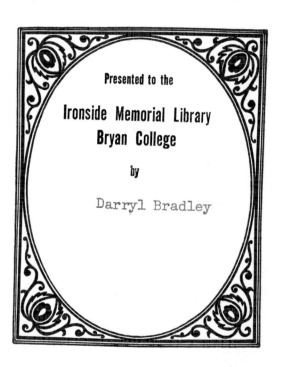

19-12

THE STORY WITHOUT AN END

BY WILLIAM A CHAPMAN

Published By:
The World Home Bible League
16801 Van Dam Road
South Holland, Illinois 60473

Printed in U.S.A.

44578

FROM THE AUTHOR

I do not claim that this book is a literary masterpiece, for I am not a professional author, but it is my personal testimony concerning the power and presence of God in my life and in the lives of others.

During the history of the World Home Bible League thousands of you have stood by us faithfully with your gifts and prayers and have helped make the World Home Bible League what it is today. Many times I have wished that I could sit down with you to share what God has done in our lives; but this is impossible. One way in which I felt it could be done was through a book. Therefore, my wife and I have underwritten the entire first edition in an attempt to share with you the miracles God has performed in the history of the World Home Bible League. The first 50,000 copies will be given free of charge to those who have supported us with their gifts and prayers. They are given with the prayer that God will continue to inspire you and all others to even greater efforts in the distribution of God's Word around the world.

Most sincerely yours,
William A. Chapman

FROM THE PUBLISHER

The entire first edition of this book (50,000 copies) has been underwritten by Mr. and Mrs. William A. Chapman. The publisher has been given this edition for distribution to those who have contributed to the work of the World Home Bible League.

The World Home Bible League has ordered another printing available to all who wish to order additional copies to share with their friends. They are available on the basis of a contribution of $1.00. Special consideration will be given to large orders for distribution to Sunday schools, Societies, etc. All contributions exceeding the cost of these books will be used in the general ministry of the World Home Bible League.

World Home Bible League
16801 Van Dam Road
South Holland, Illinois 60473

INTRODUCTION

It was Good Friday afternoon, 1938. A man and a woman walked toward an obscure home in Walkerton, Indiana, and knocked on the door. They had an idea in their minds and a burden on their hearts. As the door swung open, they asked a simple question, "Do you have a Bible in your home?" The answer was no. Upon the promise that the Bible would be read Mr. and Mrs. William Chapman placed that first Bible. It was just as simple as that.

Little did these dedicated people dream that in the years that lay ahead the same episode would be repeated hundreds of thousands of times as sowers followed in their footsteps to place the Scriptures in Bibleless homes not only throughout the United States but throughout the known world.

Today, the name World Home Bible League is synonymous with mission work. Wherever there is a missionary there is the Scripture, and frequently that Bible, that Testament, or that Scripture portion is a publication of the World Home Bible League.

It would be next to impossible to give a complete resumé of how God blessed that initial call in Walkerton. It has been my privilege as director of the World Home Bible League to visit many of the fields that have received free Scriptures. At a lonely lighthouse guarding the rocky shores of Vancouver Island I found a World Home Bible

League Scripture in the hands of a lighthouse keeper. Far away in the heart of the Cuban swamplands a woman, with a broad smile on her face, showed me a little red Testament also published by the League. At a large hospital in Nigeria there was a literature table. Two-thirds of the material on that table were World Home Bible League publications. On the island of Ceylon in the well-known town of Kandy, home of the world-famous Temple of the Tooth, a former Buddhist priest received a copy of the Sinhalese Scripture provided by the Ceylon Home Bible League, and the Holy Spirit, through the Word, converted him. A criminal awaiting his execution on a scaffold in Japan testified of his faith in Christ his Saviour whom he met on the pages of a Japanese New Testament placed through our Japan affiliate. In an almost unknown tribe living on a South Sea island a man who speaks a strange dialect known only to a few hundred men received the Word of God the other day in his own language, thanks to the ministry of the Wycliffe Bible Translators and the World Home Bible League.

Our seed is the Word. It is the incorruptible Word of the very God. Our field is the world, and as we sow the seed the field becomes larger. Every day new horizons stretch out before us.

The growth pattern of the World Home Bible League has been the subject of conversation among many individuals in homes, in schools, and in seminaries. We believe the growth of this ministry was because God's hand of blessing rested upon us in every turn despite the fact that many times we were not as faithful as we should have been. Though we were not, God was.

I am sure that as you read this interesting book you will feel for the first time the motivation and the enthusiasm of our founder. These are personal testimonies from the heart of a man who has dedicated his life and his pursuit to the great task that God gave him to do. We trust that the reading of this book will be a source of inspiration and blessing to you and the challenge for you to do even greater things for God.

WILLIAM ACKERMAN, *International Director,*
World Home Bible League

DEDICATION

The theme text of the World Home Bible League is Psalm 126:5: "They that sow in tears shall reap in joy."

The symbol of our organization is the sower and it is to that individual that we dedicate this book.

The sower may live in Lagos, Nigeria, or Tokyo, Japan. In fact, he may live anywhere in this world, in one of its great cities or on some lonely island. He may be a member of any race because the sower knows no geographical boundary and no racial isolation.

The sower goes forth to sow the seed of the everlasting gospel. He goes forth with the assurance that some of the seed he plants will produce one hundredfold.

It is to the sower then that we dedicate this book, for the sower is the human instrument God uses to make this ministry successful throughout the world.

WILLIAM A. CHAPMAN

A RIDICULOUS PRAYER?

It was in 1936 that I became seriously ill. Douwe Tamminga, an elder in my church, came to visit me at the Roseland Community Hospital in Chicago. He prayed that my life might be spared and that henceforth I would be directed into the service of Christ. This appeared to be a very strange prayer. Why should God be asked to give me health and strength for such a purpose? What could I possibly do for Christ? I came to the conclusion, shortly after Mr. Tamminga. left, that this certainly was a ridiculous prayer.

But as the hours of the night wore on toward morning, it became increasingly apparent that the elder's prayer could not easily be forgotten. It was then that my commitment to God was made. If He would restore my health, I would give the strength of my body and mind in any avenue of service to which God would direct.

From that time forward this objective was to receive the predominant place in my life. The days passed swiftly and soon became months. Gradually my strength returned. The family was able to travel to the southland where I went to recuperate.

One night on entering our hotel room in Biloxi, Mississippi, my attention was drawn to a Gideon Bible lying on a bedstand. Picking it up and turning to my wife and son I asked, "How many homes do you think there are in the United States without a Bible?"

Gradually it occurred to us that perhaps we could be used by God to help supply that need. Shortly thereafter the idea that was conceived in Biloxi did emerge as a God-directed avenue of service. We began to pray more earnestly concerning the challenge left by the elder at my bedside months before. Now that "ridiculous prayer" became more meaningful in our lives.

Our family returned to Chicago and some time later the challenge God had given was explained to a pastor friend: "I would like to form an organization with the objective of placing a Bible in every Bibleless home in America upon the promise that it would be read. This idea has taken hold of me, but I don't feel qualified to take hold of it."

His reply encouraged me greatly. "I will answer you in two words - God is! Look to Him, and ways and means will be opened that will surprise you."

It was impossible to carry out a Bible-placement ministry without a fairly large quantity of Bibles available at all times. In those days my finances were not such that I could boldly go out and order the needed supply. However, after much prayer we decided that if we were going to launch out, launch out we must! In a venture of faith, mingled with some misgivings, we purchased the first thousand Bibles. It was a mountain to us. Some people wondered whether we would ever distribute that many Bibles and, frankly, there were moments I, too, wondered.

A certain man who was told that we had purchased a thousand Bibles asked, "What in the world are you going to do with them all?"

"We are going to give them away," was the reply.

"You know, people do good only for one of two reasons, either for fear of punishment, or the hope of reward," he countered.

"Fella, you haven't begun to live," I answered.

2

Now in possession of the first thousand Bibles, our next concern was where to conduct the first survey. It was then that memory brought back to us an incident that had occurred several months before.

We had a small summer home at Koontz Lake, located near Walkerton, Indiana. On a Saturday afternoon my wife Betty and I had gone to Walkerton, and while she shopped I looked for a church at which we might worship on Sunday morning. There was an interesting little church on one of the corners, but there was no sign to indicate the time of worship, the denomination, or the pastor. After making several inquiries concerning the time of the service, we were finally given the necessary information and we attended that church the following Sunday.

Returning to our cottage immediately after the service, we discussed the message of the morning, and decided to make a personal call on the pastor.

He welcomed me into the parsonage. The conversation centered upon the morning service and the attendance.

I remarked, "Our family was at your service this morning. You certainly had a wonderful message. It is too bad that everyone in this town could not have been there. They certainly would have been blessed by your sermon."

The pastor seemed very pleased with the compliment.

I continued talking to him. "It was a surprise to me that there were so few people in the service this morning. Have you met every family in this community as yet?"

He quickly replied, "Well, no, I have been here for only eight months."

I asked him, "How many families actually live in this town?"

He answered, "About 245."

I concluded, "Well, it is probably your fault then that you do not have more people in your church. If you were in the real estate and insurance business you would find it necessary to contact at least ten homes a day. Following that schedule every family in this community would be reached within thirty days. It might also be necessary, in order to reach the businessmen of this town, that you spend additional hours soliciting their interest and patronage. If we businessmen did not follow such a practice we would probably starve to death. That is exactly why the cause of Jesus Christ is not going forward or making any impact in many areas.

"I noticed there is no sign in front of your church. If a new businessman came to this town he would erect a bulletin board explaining what kind of business it was, the hours the new venture would be open and the hours it would be closed. He might invite people to come in and get acquainted."

Because the pastor was a man of God he accepted the advice in the spirit in which it was given. Before leaving him with a word of encouragement, I told him to order a bulletin board for his church and send the bill to me. He did, and for many years the people of the town knew what the name of the church was and when the services were held.

THE FIRST CANVASS

Our experience with the pastor at Walkerton helped us decide where our first canvass would take place. On that Good Friday afternoon in 1938 my wife and I began calling on the 245 homes in Walkerton. That day forty-five families were found who had no Bible. They readily promised to read the Scripture and forty-five families received free Bibles. There was no longer any doubt in our minds as to the need of bringing the Scripture to the doorsteps of homes all across America. We also learned that afternoon the importance of encouraging those who

4

already had a Bible to take it from the mantel and to make it the centerpiece of their homes. Many others were encouraged to take their Bibles from the trunk or out of the attic.

That evening when we returned to our home we were tired but confident that God was encouraging us in the challenge He had set before us. We had begun, though in a very small way, to ask families in the U.S.A., "Do you have a Bible in your home?"

Before us was an uncharted road; where it led we did not know at that time, nor do we know today, for the story of Bible distribution through the ministries of the American Home Bible League and later the World Home Bible League is truly a "Story Without an End!"

EARLY EXPERIENCES

Although I was born in Chicago, I grew to manhood on a farm near Blue Island, Illinois. Blue Island, therefore, had a special appeal and was one of the first cities to be selected for a canvass. A pastor was contacted and the plan was explained to him. He was told that Bibles were available for every Bibleless home in Blue Island and that all he needed was volunteer workers consecrated to the task of placing them. If the pastor was willing to call together the workers who would be willing to visit every family, I promised to supply the Bibles.

The pastor inquired suspiciously, "Are you sure there are no strings attached to this offer?"

We assured him that there were no strings attached, explaining that our purpose was to share the Bible. It had been a lamp unto our feet and a light to our pathway and, therefore, we felt that we wanted to share it with others.

He readily agreed then to call together a special meeting of the ministerial association and asked me to address it.

Now, I was not a public speaker. My experience was very limited and I doubted whether the invitation would really be confirmed. I thought he probably was just stalling or trying to be nice. Much to my surprise, however, a phone call came some time later and an opportunity to address the pastors was laid right on my doorstep. Before us was a new door and we accepted this as an indication of God's blessing. Somewhat reluctantly, I, a real estate man, made the presentation to the ministerial group. My first challenge ever presented to such a group was accepted. Subsequently, every home in that city was visited by volunteer workers!

The prayer at my bedside in the Roseland Community Hospital, together with the thrill of God's leading in the canvasses at Walkerton and Blue Island, encouraged us to set even higher goals. We began to feel the need of a closer-knit organization of interested men. A call went out and a number responded. We were highly elated. However, we were soon to learn that although many are called, few are chosen. In fact, some of those who seemed to be the most enthusiastic fell by the wayside for one reason or another. But God did send us many faithful friends who have been with us through the years of the Bible League's ministry.

One day a local printer was approached with a brochure that we had prepared. The man was Chester L. Evers, Sr., with whom I had worked in my home church. Mr. Evers took the material and read it. The Spirit moved him to offer his assistance on the project. We have faithfully worked shoulder-to-shoulder from the early days of the League to the writing of this book. During this period Mr. Evers became vice-president of the League, serving many years in that capacity. Later he became president and today serves as chairman of our international board.

We began to think in terms of a name for the ministry. After much deliberation and prayer we accepted the name, American Home Bible League. A leader of one of the denominations, upon hearing the name we had chosen, laughingly said, "Whom do those people think they are anyhow, calling themselves the American Home Bible League? That is ridiculous; they have canvassed only Walkerton, Blue Island, and a few other towns. Why don't

7

they get the name in line with what they have done and call it the Chicago or Indiana Home Bible League?"

That leader had a very limited vision of what God was going to do with the ministry and, if confessions are in order, so did I.

Weeks later a letter was received from a Mr. Bell, pastor of a Congregational Church in Toulon, Illinois, and brother of a pastor in Blue Island. The letter inquired about the possibility of distributing Bibles there. Upon his invitation, a visit was made to the pastors of Toulon. Considerable discussion had already taken place, but the final decision was made at this meeting. The ministerial group would proceed with the canvass, following the same procedure used in Blue Island.

The meeting closed and the men were about to leave. Coats had been put on and their hats were in their hands. It was then a strange feeling came over me. It seemed as though the Lord was saying, "Just a moment now, don't you need Me any more?" The Scripture text, "You can do nothing without me," seemed to come back to me again and again. Then I realized that we had not even prayed about this canvass and that great decisions had been made without asking the Lord's help. But, should a layman voice his opinion on this subject to a group of pastors? The Lord led me to suggest prayer and I did not wait for an answer, but began to pray immediately, asking for God's blessing upon all the business that had been transacted. Mr. Bell, in whose home the meeting was held, began to sob audibly.

When the prayer was completed he confessed, "I have never been put to shame as I have this afternoon. The fact that we should come here as a group of clergymen to make these important decisions and not pray is almost unbelievable. That a layman should remind us of this is embarrassing, but the reminder was certainly needed."

8

Turning to me he asked, "Brother, will you take my church service next Sunday?" Somewhat stunned, I replied, "No, I will not be able to make it."

He began pressing me for another date, but I was evasive, feeling unqualified to accept his offer. Looking back now, I realized how gracious and how patient God was with me. Although an unworthy steward at times, He had already begun to prove His faithfulness in my life and future ministry.

GOD SENDS THE RIGHT MAN

During the early days of the ministry we made many personal calls on pastors to acquaint them with our work. One day I was sitting in my car on the north side of Chicago in front of an old church building checking a directory.

A man who noticed the car came over and asked, "Is there anything I can do for you?" He introduced himself as the Reverend Sam McDill, explaining that he was the minister of that church which had just reopened after being closed for a long period of time. He related in glowing terms how he looked forward to developing the Sunday School and was already holding regular services in that church. He told me that already the results were very encouraging.

Then I explained the American Home Bible League's ministry to him and told him of the burden God had given us. He replied that he had already heard something about our work and had intended to call us. He invited us to come to address his congregation the following Sunday. This offer was accepted with gratitude. We felt that God had definitely led us to this interesting interview with the right man who, in turn, was used by God to lead us to still others.

WE MEET DR. IRONSIDE

Rev. Sam McDill offered to introduce us to Dr. Harry Ironside. The meeting took place at the Moody Church at eleven o'clock in the morning. Dr. Ironside greeted us, and during the interview I had the opportunity to give my personal testimony. Dr. Ironside seemed to be impressed by what God had done in my life and in the ministry of the newly formed American Home Bible League.

Thus far Dr. Ironside was the best known pastor that we had ever contacted about our ministry. He was very influential and was a saint of God. I was surprised when he proposed, "Mr. Chapman, we intend to hold our Sunday school banquet and for the first time in the history of Moody Church we have not announced who the speaker will be. Already the announcements have gone out, but somehow we didn't announce who would bring the message. This must be God's leading. Will you address our Sunday school teachers?" God had opened another door.

After this experience Dr. Ironside telephoned and explained that he would like to launch a canvass from the Moody Church in Chicago. This was a fantastic challenge, beyond our fondest expectations. Dr. Ironside explained that he would like to form a large cross with Bibles in front of the pulpit. He asked whether we would be willing to send 1,500 Bibles and told us that half the time of the service would be allotted to us. Through this opportunity our cause could be presented to those gathered in the church while countless thousands would be listening over the radio network.

That Sunday we awakened early. The assignment at Moody Church, which included the broadcast, was a very formidable one for me. But I had promised to go and so, reluctantly, we made our way to the church. A typewritten copy of my message had been prepared in the event it would be required by Dr. Ironside. When the written copy was presented to him he said, "Mr Chapman, you are not required to give me a copy of what you are going to say. I was at the Sunday school teachers' banquet and we were most pleased to note the way the Spirit of the Lord led you. I am sure that He will do so again this morning."

Dr. Ironside was absolutely right. As I stood behind the pulpit of the great Moody Church and thought of the well-known Bible teachers who had occupied that place of honor, I was acutely aware of my own limitations. I felt deeply dependent upon the Holy Spirit for leading and I must confess that it was only through this divine help that the assignment was successfully completed.

One Sunday some time later, teams of workers went out into the area surrounding Moody Church. Two by two they visited the homes of men and women, inviting them to come to church, to tune in to the radio, to come out to Sunday school, or send their children. Thousands of homes were contacted. Many Bibles were placed upon the promise that they would be read. Some months later it was reported that at a Sunday service in the church a man stood up and told how some workers had called at his home and had invited him to the Moody Church. Holding a Bible high he said that it was through the preaching at the Moody Church and through the reading of that Bible given to him through the American Home Bible League that he met Jesus Christ.

We do not know the complete story resulting from this conversion, but this we know, people came to church, children came to Sunday school, and at least one soul was saved for Christ.

A STAB OF REMORSE

The assignment at Moody Church served as an

encouraging stimulant for the tasks assigned to us later. Each new assignment testified to the fact that the Lord had blessed and led and allowed us successfully to complete the assignment. I gained more confidence. Then I remembered the incident that had occurred many years before in Toulon, Illinois, when the pastor placed before me the first invitation to accept a church service. I remembered vividly that it had been turned down, and a stab of remorse filled me.

I wrote the pastor offering to speak at his church. Only a few days passed and a letter from the pastor's wife arrived at my home. I tore open the envelope, unfolded the letter, and was shocked to read, "We buried Reverend Bell yesterday." The truth seemed to shout at me. This opportunity was now forever gone. I felt the necessity of talking to God again. This time another promise was made that whatever door opened in the future it would be entered with complete trust in the Lord and would be accepted as a challenge from Him. I must confess there have been times when it was very difficult to keep this promise. There were a few times when I wavered. Assignments that came our way staggered us, but by God's grace we accepted them and we shall continue to enter into all open doors, resting heavily upon God's promises.

AN EARLY DISTRIBUTION

In the very first years of the American Home Bible League's ministry we decided to send a Bible to the President of the United States. We also sent a Bible to each member of his cabinet and to each senator. Sixty-seven letters of appreciation and acknowledgment were received. One recipient admitted that there was no copy of the Scriptures in his office library until this Bible was received. He expressed his gratitude to us and said that the Bible would be in his office from this time on.

One man wrote, "I appreciate the Bible and will do my very best to carry out the suggestions placed on the inside cover. I will endeavor to read a portion of the Word every day."

The first piece of literature published by the American Home Bible League accompanied these Bibles. It was a booklet with pictures of past presidents. The booklet also included statements that were made by great men regarding the Bible. On the back cover were these words, "In colonial days every school was a little Bible institute. The content of the New England primer, the standard school reader for possibly 150 years, was 7/8's Bible. It may be said that the early American was a man of one book, the Bible, but that is no longer true. Today the reading of the Bible in many homes has now become a lost art, whereas, in the early history of our country the average family built its home upon the rock, the Word of God. America must return to the Bible."

For many years this popular little booklet was the one and only promotional piece we had. It was highly effective and helped open many doors for Bible distribution.

A PASTOR AND TWELVE COMMUNISTS

The telephone in the office of the chief of police at Elizabeth, New Jersey, rang. The police officer picked up the phone and a cheerful voice at the other end of the wire advised him that it was Pastor Willard Crunkleton of the Christian and Missionary Alliance Church.

"I have just finished reading the *Elizabeth Journal.* There is a story in it about twelve Communists who were arrested for distributing subversive literature at the Singer Sewing Machine plant. According to the story they are going to be arraigned tomorrow. Would you please permit me to speak to them for about ten minutes? I have something important to tell them."

The chief of police knew that dynamic Pastor Crunkleton would not take no for an answer. What could he do but graciously grant the pastor's request?

The following morning the twelve Communists were lined up in a room. Special guards and policemen were also there. Pastor Crunkleton walked in, quickly introduced himself and gave a ten-minute sermonette. The Holy Spirit used the message to startle the Communists as well as the policemen. With a straight-from-the-shoulder delivery he told the prisoners that at best they were a disillusioned lot and that only one thing would ever straighten out their warped minds. "What you need," declared Brother Crunkleton, "is a conscientious, prayerful reading of the Word of God. You need a Bible in your home. Although you will probably be in a jail cell for some time to come, it will be all that you can call home, and I propose to offer everyone of you a copy of the Holy Scripture."

At this point Mr. Crunkleton gave a signal. From the other room a dignified Lutheran clergyman, dressed in his black garb, ceremoniously wheeled in a typewriter table. On the table were twelve copies of the World Home Bible League Scripture. They were offered to the prisoners and one by one the Communists accepted them. Some even muttered a "thank you." They were then hustled away in a patrol wagon to begin a prison term.

Reporting this incident later to the League the pastor wrote, "Perhaps I transgressed one of your rules. I could not ask the Communists to promise to read it, but I still think it was an effective placement. Four days later I saw a picture in the daily newspaper of these men being ushered into an armored truck and I noticed several of them carrying the Bibles."

The chief of police called Mr. Crunkleton some time later to say that this was a most impressive event, one that he would remember for a long time in his career as a policeman. Pastor Crunkleton sowed the seed of the Word in a city courtroom confident that "The Word of God is quick and powerful and sharper than any two-edged sword."

A THOUSAND AND ONE THINGS FREE

My son Herman and our director, Mr. Ackerman, were returning from Japan. This was back in the days when there were only propeller aircraft, and the plane stopped to refuel at the Hawaiian Islands. Looking over the magazines and books that were offered for sale at the airport they spied a book, *One Thousand and One Things Free*. On the front cover was a list of the things you could get free and, believe it or not, it said, "Free Bible, Page 101." They looked up the reference and there on page 101 it said, "Free Bibles to Bibleless homes, write to the World Home Bible League, 425 West 107 Street, Chicago, Illinois," which was our address at that time. Although we had not authorized this to be put in the book, someone had put it there. We received many written requests for Bibles as a result of that unsolicited advertisement.

A MOST UNUSUAL NEWSPAPER

One year we began receiving a very large number of requests and each of these requests, handwritten, mentioned a newspaper that was printed in the Detroit area. Somewhat perplexed we decided to look into the matter because the requests amounted to hundreds. Finally we were able to trace the newspaper and asked the publisher to send us two copies of it. It was a newspaper that fed the appetites of those who indulged in filth and pornography.

Inside this distasteful newspaper was a small advertisement which read: "If you do not have a Bible in your home, write to ---" and gave our name and address.

We had no idea who was responsible for the advertisement. At first we planned to throw away all the letters. But a pastor friend said, "As I remember, there is a story in the Bible that Jesus sat down and ate with sinners and when He was criticized for this He said, 'I came into the world to save sinners.' Where could you get a better market to place your Bibles than among people of this type? These are the ones who need the Bible." We compromised and sent each one a New Testament. Who can tell what light shone in their dark lives as a result?

SOME EARLY PERSONAL INCIDENTS

WITNESSING TO A FORMER EMPLOYER

Before entering the real estate business I was a sales representative of a national office machine company for four years. After leaving that concern, I had a great burden to witness to my former sales manager.

There wasn't a great deal of fellowship between the men and myself while I was employed there. Many of them gambled and drank and this was obnoxious to me, but, because of lack of courage on my part at that time, I did not give them a clear-cut Christian witness.

However, as God began proving Himself in the ministry, and as spiritual things became more real to me, this burden became heavier. It was then I felt that I should once again meet with Mr. K., the sales manager, who was in charge of a Brooklyn, New York, office. On one occasion when I was in New York City, I took a taxicab to Brooklyn and went to his office. I gave his receptionist my card and was ushered into his office. A look of surprise appeared on his face.

"Chapman, I never expected to see you again. Sit down," he said.

My former boss placed his head in his hands, looked right into my eyes, as he had done in the past, and shocked me with, "Tell me frankly, Chapman, what the hell brought you to Brooklyn?"

The crude language he used so often in days past

startled me, but I replied, *"You* have brought me to Brooklyn. I came to tell you that all the success you have is not worth the paper it is written on. You could just as well toss it into the bottom of the Hudson River. I am here to talk to you about your soul."

He looked me over carefully and finally said, with another oath, "You always were different."

Placing a copy of the Scripture before him and pointing out several verses, I asked him to think about them and to pray that God might reveal Himself to him.

As we parted, there were tears in his eyes and tears in mine. His farewell was, "Chapman, you must have some love in your heart for me and I am grateful for your concern."

It seemed as though my burden rolled away after that interview. Less than two months later one of his associates wrote me that the sales manager had died suddenly. But apparently during the last couple of months of his life he had completely mellowed. "It seemed as if something had changed him," the writer said. Results are not our business. It is our responsibility only to sow the Word of God, to bring a Christian witness, and God will bring the results. Perhaps that's just what God did with Mr. K.

TAKING THE MILK OUT OF KIDS' MOUTHS

I was the president of a service organization in our community. We had sponsored work for underprivileged children and had a good year. During September a problem arose. It concerned a project for raising funds to provide milk for orphaned children. The controversy arose because the club wanted to sponsor the project on the following two Sunday afternoons. The chairman of the committee who called me about this project said, "We ought to raise thousands of dollars through this effort."

I explained that although I was very much in favor of

the project itself it was against my convictions to have such a drive on Sunday. I explained further that if it were to be held on any of the other six days of the week it would carry my endorsement, but as a Sunday activity, I, as chairman, could not approve it.

An hour later I walked into the local bank. Two gentlemen from our club were there. One of them sarcastically remarked, "I understand you are trying to take the milk out of kids' mouths."

"No," I told him, "that is not the case. In fact, in order to prove my sincerity I will give $200 to the milk fund if you will give $50 each." They looked at each other. Neither was willing to give the $50.

This was the first opportunity that forced me to take a stand publicly in the community for my convictions. A few hours later I went to the local publisher to bring some advertisements for my business affairs. Another member of the club was there and said, "I am placing an article in the paper stating that we are sponsoring this local project on the next two Sundays."

"You have no right to publish that at this time," I told him. "We are going to have another meeting this afternoon. If the plan is accepted, you can print the article and also announce my resignation as president of the club."

A tense atmosphere existed in the meeting. Congratulating the committee on the plan that had been set up and explaining that I would be for it on any other day but Sunday, I mentioned that although Voltaire had never been of much inspiration to me, I agreed with one statement attributed to him: "I disapprove of what you say, but I will defend to the death your right to say it." I then asked them to give me that same right.

The matter was discussed heatedly for some time.

Finally someone suggested that we respect the views of the president. Later, a majority of the men stood in line to shake hands. Not all of them were in agreement with me, but they seemed to appreciate the stand I had taken.

It was interesting to note some of the developments that resulted from this incident. God inclined the man in the newspaper office to buy the highest-priced home in our community from my agency. For many years we handled many of his business affairs. The man who wanted to place the article in the paper had been associated with another real estate office. In November of that same year he approached our office and indicated a desire to work for us. He began work on January 1, 1935 and has been with us ever since.

Isn't it interesting how the real problems of life sometimes turn out to be the greatest blessing? The Scripture's promise is ever true, "All things work together for good" (Romans 8:28, RSV), but how many times we find ourselves neglecting to put faith in that sure promise.

A MAN IN NEED

A gentleman came into my office one Monday morning. He had gone through some really deep waters, which was evident from his appearance, for he looked like a physical wreck. As we engaged in conversation concerning spiritual things it became apparent to me that this man was under deep conviction. He told how he could not find rest or peace of mind. He explained that he had rented a cottage in Minnesota for a month in an attempt to relax, but he had remained for only ten days. He summed up his story by saying, "I am absolutely at the end of my rope, I have come to you this morning for help."

I told him, "I do not know whether I can help you or not, but I can introduce you to Someone who can." Bowing my head I began to pray.

Shortly afterwards he asked, "If I give my heart to Christ now will my mother know about it?" He had had a godly mother, and had known the way because she had taught it to him.

I told him, "I cannot promise you that your mother will know if you give Christ your heart, but the Bible says that the angels in heaven rejoice over one sinner that repents."

He surrendered his heart and life to the Lord that morning and, as far as I know, he has been living a Christian life now for many years.

When he was asked why he came to my office, he answered, "At the annual banquet of the Kiwanis organization you installed some new members and at the time you gave a meaningful Christian witness I have not forgotten. I have watched you for many years and I have always felt that you had something I lacked."

It is my prayer that this may always be true of my life. I trust your prayer is that it may be true in your life also.

A PASTOR RESPONDS

One day while driving through a small town in northern Illinois, our attention was focused upon a church set on a hill. Something about the church aroused my interest. It seemed to present a good opportunity for the work of the World Home Bible League's ministry, and we stopped and knocked at the door of the parsonage.

The pastor graciously invited us into the home and we told him the burden that was upon our hearts. But he answered, "I am afraid that I am not interested. We are now getting along well with all the other pastors and I don't want to be crossing wires by calling on different homes in the community. This just doesn't appeal to me. I am living in peace with the rest of the pastors and I am satisfied."

I answered, "You are paying a very high price for peace. There are people all around you who are going to hell while you are living in peace. I am placing these Bibles in your lap, Pastor. The prayer in my heart is that you will place them in the homes of your community and display the love which I am sure you preach from your pulpit."

The pastor did not seem overjoyed over the project and perhaps this was understandable. However, several months later a letter came from him saying that he had placed one of the Bibles within a stone's throw of his parsonage and it had led the family to church and to Christ. This had given him a new power in his pulpit. Later, in gratitude for the opportunity to distribute the Word, he invited us to conduct his morning and afternoon services, during which we were offered an opportunity to tell still more people about the growing ministry.

THE GOLDEN RULE IS NOT ENOUGH

A representative of the Internal Revenue Service called at our real estate office for an audit of our books. After spending considerable time going over the business records, he concluded, "It appears from your tax return that you are a religious man." Then before there was an opportunity to answer him, he continued, "Would you care to know what my religion is? My religion is the Golden Rule."

Surprised at the man's frankness, I answered, "As wonderful as the Golden Rule is, my friend, it cannot take you all the way and it won't. Apart from the Lord Jesus Christ there can be no salvation."

The agent looked at me thoughtfully and said, "I wonder what can be up. Just last evening my mother, who is seventy-nine years of age, took me to task. She was disappointed in my lack of interest in spiritual things. Now I meet you this morning during a tax audit and once again
22

I am involved in the subject of religion."

I suggested, "What you should do, young man, is to take time right now and thank God for your mother. It is wonderful to have a mother who is praying for you and who has real concern for your spiritual welfare."

"I will acknowledge that I am not content with life and that something definitely seems to be missing," he confessed.

"Apart from Jesus Christ," I assured him, "there is no happiness, nor is there peace of heart or mind. One cannot possibly be happy without faith."

The importance of a Christian testimony to men we meet in all walks of life can never be overemphasized.

TESTIMONY TO THE JUDGE

One day I was asked to testify in court. This appearance concerned a bill that was presented to the legislature. It dealt with the Sunday closing of business houses. The matter had become a debatable issue in our community. Opinions were sharply divided. The judge asked how many years I had been in business. "Twenty-five years and, regardless of the outcome of this bill, my place of business will be closed on Sunday. It always has been and it will continue to be so. These are my convictions and the decision rendered on this bill will have no bearing on my future operations. With me, Sunday closing is a settled matter," I explained.

The judge's interest was definitely aroused. He probed, "You have been successful in your business, is that right?"

"Your honor," I replied, "my door is still open for business every day except Sunday. They tell me when you have your door open for business you are considered to be successful."

The judge commented, "I want you to know that it is very refreshing to me to have a man in my court this morning who has the convictions that you express and I am happy to learn that, despite the fact that your business is closed on Sunday, you continue to be successful in your field."

MELTING OPPOSITION

Early in the League's ministry a local pastor seemed to be opposed to our ministry. He was a wonderful servant of God and held in high regard in the community. Although I was very disappointed at his opposition, I realized that it was because he knew so little of us and what we were attempting to do. It was our desire to reach others through the printed page. He could not help being in favor of our ministry, but still he seemed to be in opposition. I think God was teaching me a lesson. It was that I should not be too concerned over opposition.

I received a letter from him. It stated that the work of the World Home Bible League must be of the Lord. In addition to other complimentary remarks a check for $300 was enclosed. I have always been thankful for this lesson, thankful that God gave grace during these years of opposition to commend this problem to Him and that He melted the opposition.

THE USHER WHO BECAME A DEACON

A man accompanied me to a meeting one evening in a small town in Iowa and as we were about to retire for the evening he stated, "My heart was stirred and challenged tonight. I would like to make my life count for Christ."

I answered, "I am sure that you are serious. You should begin by telling God what you just told me. God does not need any of us but in His wonderful providence He uses His followers to accomplish His divine purposes. If you will tell God of your desire and claim daily the promise of Psalm 37:4, 'Delight thyself also in the Lord; and he shall give thee the desires of thine heart,' then God will open

24

the door for you."

Some time later my friend came into my office. He was bubbling over. "They have asked me to be an usher at the church," he confided. Three months later the church burned down. It was decided that the church services would be held at the local school. There was a need for a dedicated worker and the man was asked to be there early on Sunday morning to place the Bibles, the pulpit, the hymnbooks, and arrange all the chairs. He was happy in his new assignment. When the new building was dedicated once again he could not wait to tell me that he had now been asked to be the head usher. He told me that he was praying that the Lord would help him to be the best usher there ever was.

This is the kind of dedication, the kind of men that are needed in the church; men you can count on to do the very best no matter what their task may be.

A PROPHETIC UTTERANCE

During the first four years of our ministry we did not present the work of the League at our home church or in our immediate locality. Perhaps God led us in this decision. We felt that we should carry on the work outside of our own circle of friends. We did so to determine its real need and to test whether or not people would respond to our program. Several articles began to appear in various Christian journals and some of our local people then began to ask, "What's going on? What in the world are you doing?"

It was on Thanksgiving, 1942, four years after we started that the story of the League was first presented in our home church. On that evening I made the statement, "I believe that some day God's people will respond and more than $100,000 will be received for the work of the League."

25

Afterward I wondered whether the statement was a wise one. One hundred thousand dollars was a large sum of money and just the thought of obtaining that budget caused us to tremble. However, during the next few days God inclined the hearts of His people to send more than $1,600 to my home. We were grateful to God for the encouragement that helped make these prophetic utterances come true. Our International Board, in the year of 1969, adopted a budget for the year of 1970 which was in excess of one million dollars. How grateful we are to Him "that is able to do exceedingly abundantly above all we ask or think according to the power that worketh in us."

A SMALL MEETING BRINGS BIG DIVIDENDS

In 1941, Bill Ackerman, a young businessman, was elected president of the mission society in his church in Paterson, New Jersey. He accepted this new responsibility seriously and attempted to discharge it as effectively as possible. The Rev. William Haverkamp had come to the Paterson area from a pastorate in Chicago and the new mission society president invited the pastor to address the group.

Rev. Haverkamp accepted the invitation and gave a very informative and challenging message. He used as the basis of his message the fact that the three-year-old American Home Bible League was organized a short distance from his former church and it was, as the pastor indicated, a good way in which to get people involved in Christian witnessing. Perhaps, suggested the speaker, the League's founder, William Chapman, would be willing to come to New Jersey and tell of his experiences. When it was discovered that Mr. Chapman would travel at his own expense, Mr. Ackerman felt that he had not too much to lose and so the invitation was given.

The meeting was promoted in many ways and efforts were made to enlist the aid of every member of the newly formed mission society. Mr. Chapman had written that he would speak and show a film. Those were the days when motion pictures and films were not too well received and some churches would not allow even religious films to be shown in the auditorium. At the last moment permission was given, but only forty-two people attended the showing and Mr. Ackerman was deeply embarrassed.

However, from that small gathering came many blessings. It resulted in the first Bible canvass of Paterson. Subsequent canvasses covered more than 12,000 homes, and hundreds of Bibles were placed.

Many new volunteer workers had been enlisted for the League. Some of them kept the program alive in that area for many years and some are still active.

One of these outstanding men was Mr. Bill Meines who for many years supervised the collections from world banks on the Eastern seaboard.

The greatest result as I look back upon this experience was the burden that was laid upon Mr. Ackerman's heart, a burden so pressing that the promotion of the American Home Bible League became his major concern. A strong compulsion seized him one day that he should take a more active part in our ministry. A businessman in the East, hearing of this desire, offered to underwrite his salary for one year. Mr. Ackerman began representing the League on the East Coast and then in 1951 he became the League's second international director succeeding the Rev. Spencer De Jong. Under his ministry the League grew to its present scope as an international organization.

FIFTEEN EMPTY PAGES

In 1956 the League initiated the printing of its first Spanish Testament. The text was set and the number of plates involved came to 231. Those who are familiar with book manufacturing know that books are made up in signatures and you cannot have an uneven number of pages. Therefore, fifteen blank pages would have to appear in our New Testament. This seemed to be very wasteful and we had no material to put on the empty pages. We did not care to add any explanations to the text. Finally, when it was almost time for the Testaments to be printed it occurred to us to fill these pages with well-known Spanish hymns. Among those suggested were, "Jesus Saves," "Trust and Obey," "Holy, Holy, Holy," etc. These were added and the Testaments went to press. Copies soon filtered down into Mexico and Cuba. It was then we discovered that this was truly a leading of the Holy Spirit. Hymnbooks were almost entirely unknown in some of these areas of the Spanish-speaking world and ours were one of the most popular Testaments ever distributed in the Latin world. Many times we recall with fond memories listening to the congregation singing out of their little red Testaments the familiar hymns of the Christian church.

One of the most popular hymns of all is "When The Roll Is Called Up Yonder I'll Be There." It is hard to beat the great enthusiasm displayed by Spanish-speaking people as they sing this great hymn of the church of Jesus Christ. Every time we heard them sing and watched their faces glow with an inner warmth and fervor, it left little doubt in our minds that when the roll is called up yonder they will be there.

A SUSPICIOUS NEIGHBOR

During the history of the World Home Bible League, representatives have presented programs in thousands of churches throughout the United States and Canada. Many of these were located within driving distance of Chicago. Many times I have spoken to such church groups. As a result, quite often I came home late in the evening and sometimes early the following morning.

One afternoon, expecting a large shipment of Scriptures to be delivered to my home and knowing that I would not be there, a neighbor was asked whether he would kindly open the door to my basement and allow the trucker to deliver the Bibles. He agreed to do so.

Some years later the neighbor informed me that for a long time he was very suspicious about my coming home so late at night. He couldn't figure out what I was doing so late at night and so early in the morning. When he discovered that I was out speaking in the interest of Bibleless homes, which became apparent to him when I asked him to open my home for the Bible delivery, he admitted that he was ashamed he had been so suspicious.

THE LORD PROVIDES FOR HIS WORK AND WORKERS

A series of meetings were held in the eastern part of our country, the last of these at the Abbey Reformed Church in Clymer, New York. The church is located about 100 miles from Rochester and train reservations had been obtained for me. However, there was an unusually heavy snowstorm and all the through trains to New York City were late. The only transportation available was a local train. I was burdened down with a suitcase, a six-foot screen, a motion picture projector, and a phonograph that gave the musical accompaniment for the film. Needless to say it was next to impossible for me to board the train. The conductor, after surveying my plight, emphatically stated, "You cannot take all this equipment with you in the coach." I was determined to do so and boarded the train. To my utter amazement and gratitude there were two empty seats facing each other. All the equipment was placed on one seat and there was still ample room to sit on the opposite side. The train pulled out of the station with every other seat in that coach filled. God had shown evidence of going before in providing for His work and His worker.

A DEAD MISSION SOCIETY COMES TO LIFE

A pastor of an Indiana church at which I was asked to speak stated upon my arrival, "We appreciate the challenge you gave at one of our former churches. When we came here my wife and I decided to ask you to present the challenge at our mission society meeting. This society is dead and we have got to put some new life into it. One thing we do not want to do, however, is to go out and canvass the community."

My reply was this: "Pastor, you have been very frank and I should like to be as frank with you. It is impossible ever to have a spark in a mission society while there is no concern, love, or compassion for souls outside of the church. Suppose we go into your study. We will pray and ask God that everything that should be said here tonight will be said and that He will keep us from saying what should not be said." He agreed and together we prayed that God would direct us and help bring the right emphasis.

At the meeting I spoke concerning the lethargy of many who sit in the church without any apparent concern for the lost souls of men. I urged the members to go out and call at the home of their neighbors inviting them to church and Sunday school and offering a free Scripture wherever the promise was made that it would be read. There was deep interest. A Bible canvass was carried out and a dead mission society rejuvenated.

A GREAT MISSIONARY ASKS A FAVOR

Many years ago I was asked to go to the Chicago loop to meet Dr. Samuel Zwemer, the well-known missionary to

Arabia. After meeting him in Chicago I returned to the Roseland suburb and brought him to the pastor's home. As he left the car he asked, "Would you do me a favor? Would you pray for me? I don't really feel up to the challenge that is facing me this morning."

This shook me up because here was a man God had so greatly used in His service; a man who had spent many years for the Lord in Arabia. Yet this great missionary of the church not only felt the need of prayer, but had asked me to pray for him. Many times I have thought over this incident and know now why God has so greatly used this man in the service of Christ.

A WORD OF ENCOURAGEMENT

We were encouraged to approach a large denomination to ask for its support on a denomination-wide basis. Some who were vitally interested in the World Home Bible League were prepared to present this request through a committee at the annual business session.

When we arrived at the hotel where the meeting was to be held, we were advised that there was a great deal of agitation and opposition. This came, surprisingly enough, from another Bible distribution agency in its attempt to prevent the denomination from giving us its full support. A conference was set up and representatives from the other Bible agency and some committee members asked me to meet with them. One of the men present asked, "So you are looking for recognition?"

"I am certainly not looking for any recognition for myself. But I don't apologize for seeking recognition on behalf of our ministry," I answered. "That is why I'm here and at my own expense."

The discussion became rather heated and finally one of the committee members said, "I propose to do everything I can for Mr. Chapman and the World Home Bible League.

Certainly this cannot be considered competition. I believe that this cause is entitled to recognition and support."

The next morning I was asked to address the meeting of all the representatives present. After my message one of the ministers took me by the arm and led me to the rear of the auditorium. He asked me to look over the landscape through a picture window and he observed, "Do you see how nice and green the grass is out there?"

I could not help saying, "Yes."

He countered, "Remember, it didn't get that way from one shower. Keep pitching and your cause will continue to grow and be recognized in our circles and in many others."

God knows what encouragement we need and I have found that He always supplies it when it is needed. I can testify in words from the Scripture, "Great is thy faithfulness."

NUMBER 9

A large number 9 tag is tied on the radio knob in my car. Many people inquire what it represents. When one gentleman asked I answered, "Frankly, that number 9 is to remind me of something that is very, very personal.

"In the Gospel of Luke there were ten men who stood afar off and cried to the Lord. It wasn't lawful for them to come close since they were afflicted by the terrible disease of leprosy.

"Their cry was, 'Jesus, Master, have mercy on us,' and the Lord was merciful. Now, certainly, they must all have started with a spark of faith, or they would not have gone to show themselves to the priest and be healed at Christ's command. They were all healed, but only one came and fell down at Jesus' feet thanking Him for being restored. The Lord inquired, 'Were there not ten cleansed? but where are the nine?'

"Evidently he could not answer the Lord. Perhaps he

32

felt it was none of his business. Well, it is none of my business either, but I want to make it my business.

"I too was raised from a sickbed many years ago. I have this tag here to remind me of the nine who failed to give thanks. It is my desire more than anything else in all the world to live a grateful life. I want to be thankful every day for my health, for the strength of body and mind that have been given to me, and I want to use them in the service of Christ."

The little number 9 tag has given me many opportunities for Christian testimony.

FELLOW TRAVELERS ALONG THE WAY

I am thankful that God blessed my business affairs throughout the years, which made it possible for me to travel for the ministry of the League throughout the North American continent and the world at my own expense. It has been a privilege also to have my wife join me and together share the Word of God around the world.

THE TEACHER WITHOUT A BIBLE

My wife and I arrived at our hotel in Paris. It was late and there was an elderly lady sitting in the lounge. We struck up a conversation with her and soon discovered that she was a teacher from California. She appeared to be a very frustrated individual and she openly expressed this.

Finally, I said, "Lady, you need someone outside of yourself to put your faith in."

She inquired, "Are you talking religion to me?"

I answered, "No, there is too much religion in the world today. Let's talk about a person. I want to tell you what that person means to me and what He, Jesus Christ, could mean to you. Are you familiar with the Holy Scripture?"

She answered, "No, I am not."

"You are a teacher and still you never have had a Bible?"

"That is right," she affirmed.

"Well, this is a New Testament. It is a part of the Bible and it is an unusual Testament. It is a marked edition as is indicated on the front cover. We have verses underlined

34

throughout this Testament which pertain to sin, salvation, and leading a thankful Christian life."

The Testament was placed in her hand and I asked her to look at the inside cover. "What does it say?" I inquired.

She answered, "Turn to page 313," which she did. She read aloud the underlined verse of Romans 3:23, "For all have sinned, and come short of the glory of God."

I asked her, "You are a teacher. What does this mean to you?"

She answered, "That means everyone."

"That is right," I agreed, "but we are dealing here with the sin question. It has to be settled by each of us or we will never travel the road that leads to redemption."

She retorted, "Nobody ever talked to me like that before."

"Somebody should have perhaps," I countered, and then I pointed to the bottom of the page which indicated we should turn to page 177 where she read, "The wages of sin is death..."

We talked further about sin and the need of atonement and then I explained to her that man was in need of a mediator who would stand between God and him. She willingly followed the other verses and when she finished reading them she handed the Testament back to me.

I said, "Lady, I wouldn't take that Testament away from you for anything. Take it into the quiet of your room tonight. Meditate upon those verses. Pray that God will enlighten you so that He will reveal Himself to you. I suggest that you read this book from cover to cover."

Her answer was curt. "No, when I get back to California and into the swing of teaching I won't have time for this stuff."

It was then I did a very dangerous thing; one I don't recommend to others. I told her, "Lady, at your age you better take time for this stuff."

Rather sarcastically I thought, she snapped, "I will take it and I will read it."

We visited for a little while longer and then we parted. Results are not our business. Our business is to be sowers of the Word and the promise of God that the Word will not return to Him void is good enough for me.

Three weeks later we were returning aboard ship. A woman came up to me while I was standing talking to the purser and inquired, "Didn't I meet you in Paris?"

I looked at her and answered, "No, I don't believe you did."

She asked, "Aren't you Mr. Chapman?"

It was then I began to recognize her. "Yes, you are the lady I met in the lobby of the hotel in Paris sometime ago."

She answered, "Yes, and I want to thank you for being so nasty with me. I did what you told me to do beginning that very night. I cried myself to sleep and the Christ who means so much to you has become my Saviour too. As I return to my teaching post in California the love of Christ will motivate my actions from now on."

THE PRESIDENT OF A THEOSOPHICAL COLLEGE

The World Home Bible League had sponsored a very successful program of Scripture distribution in India and more than three million families had been reached. What a thrill it was for me to visit India and meet a number of persons who were involved in carrying out the Bible distribution and correspondence program. An invitation was extended to me to give the graduation address for the nurses of Mary Lott Lyles Hospital in Madanapalle, South India. We also were offered the chapel service at a local theosophical college. Several hundred young men would be present and I would speak through an interpreter. I was told that I could present the claims of Christ to these men.

Now, for those who may not be familiar with a theosophical college, its teachings are quite different from ours. Its adherents believe that God is approachable through Buddha, or through Christ, or even through Mohammed. There are many avenues through which one may approach God.

After the chapel service I was introduced to the president of the college who spoke fluent English. As we walked into his office and sat down I said, "Mr. President, I am a builder. Many years ago I received a summons from the court. There was a lien placed against one of the first homes built by my company. This was a matter of great concern to me. It was placed in the hands of my attorney and together we went to the city hall to look up the record. We found that the lien was incorrect. The legal description was an error. It really involved the property next door to mine. However, the summons was in my name so I had to appear in court. The attorney and I walked into the courtroom. The bailiff announced a Chicago construction company versus William A. Chapman. Together with my attorney I stood before the bar of justice. A question was asked and I was about to answer. Then I realized, to my amazement, that the attorney was already speaking on my behalf."

I continued, "Mr. President, some day all of us are going to stand before the bar of justice and when that hour comes for me I thank God that I will not stand there in need of any merit of my own. As the Scripture says in the Gospel of John, 'We have an advocate with the Father.' Mr. President, it is my prayer that before you stand before this bar of justice you may search the Scripture and come to the realization that there is no other way given among men apart from the Lord Jesus Christ. Jesus said, 'I am the way, the truth, and the life.' When that hour of judgment comes, Buddha will not be there for he is dead; Mohammed will not be there for he is dead, too. Put your faith in the Living Christ."

AN OBSERVATION

Traveling to foreign countries and seeing missionaries work among the benighted people of the world gives a new vision and a new enthusiasm to win the lost for Christ. It also gives a new appreciation of all the blessings that are ours.

I firmly believe that every pastor should have the opportunity to visit a foreign mission field, not as a reward for service but as an opportunity to study the needs of men and women without Christ. We believe in a highly educated ministry and some of the pastors are the best trained in the world, but very few of them actually have the opportunity to visit a foreign country to see the spiritual need of multitudes without Christ. Ministers we have known who have visited foreign fields have come back with new vigor, enthusiasm and zeal in their pulpits and as a result have been better ambassadors for Jesus Christ. Congregations who send their pastors to see a foreign mission field do not spend money, they invest it. Businessmen who are capable and willing to provide funds for such things are wise in doing so.

GOD MOVES OUR MINISTRY TO NEW HEIGHTS

It is a wonderful thing to feel the hand of God moving in a mighty way within any work that we have undertaken for Him. Although in the early years we had very little in the way of publicity and almost next to nothing in promotional activity, still the work grew. We had only one or two staff members, and only a handful of people helped us, but it seemed that somehow or other God gave us more quality than quantity. These were times during which God moved in a mighty way to encourage us. I am sure He knew how much we needed it. Following are some of the ways in which God led us.

AMONG THE AMERICAN INDIANS (APRIL 1948)

The League has placed Bibles among many Indian tribes living in the United States. On a memorable Sunday many years ago thirty young Navajo Indians accepted the Lord Jesus Christ as their Saviour. A League Bible was placed in every one of their homes. Bibles were also placed at the Indian hospital in Rehoboth and additional Scriptures, Bibles, Testaments, and portions were distributed by missionaries on almost every Indian reservation in the United States.

FROM SOUTHERN CALIFORNIA (APRIL 1948)

The past Sunday afternoon we had thirteen teams out and we visited about 600 homes leaving a tract, a Back to God message, a Scripture Text calendar with the imprint of our church and one of your Bibles where there was

39

none. In addition to its being a blessing to those visited, it was also a great blessing to those who went out. We expect to send a contribution for your worth-while work in the future.

Reverend Boerfyn, San Diego, California

SOWING IN MAINE (FEBRUARY 1949)

We want to thank you for the Bibles and we would like more. This is a town of nearly 4,000, and from the results of the survey thus far, we are sure that there will be at least 100 Bibleless homes. Already we have found this canvass to be worthwhile. One lady accepted Christ through it, others have agreed to send their children to Sunday school, and others come to church themselves. This is a very godless area. There are many with no church connection whatever, so we are praying that this town may be won for Christ.

We shall continue to pray for your organization that through its efforts many may find Christ as their Savior.

A Rural Missionary

PORTLAND, OREGON, RECEIVES THE WORD (FEBRUARY 1949)

We acknowledge with deep gratitude receiving the twenty-eight Bibles to give out among the flood evacuees of the Guild's Lake Home Mission work among the colored people. These will be gladly received by those who lost their Bibles in the flood. As we establish classes among these 7,000 souls, these Bibles will be read.

A Grateful Sower

TORNADO VICTIMS IN ARKANSAS REACHED (FEBRUARY 1949)

At the beginning of the New Year many areas of the country were lashed by violent storms, and a tornado whipped through sections of Arkansas and Louisiana. The town of Warren, Arkansas, in the direct path of the

40

twister, felt its full fury. When the storm had passed, the town was in shambles.

Paul Harvey, one of Chicago's favorite news commentators, described the destruction on a national broadcast. The next day the Rev. Spencer De Jong, who was at that time the national director of World Home Bible League, placed a long-distance call to Mayor Jim Hurley at Warren, Arkansas. He was told only emergency calls were accepted. The operator stated there would be at least a three- to four-hour delay, but the Lord intervened and the call was completed in ten minutes. The mayor said over 200 homes were destroyed and that the city would gladly receive the shipment of Bibles. He asked if it was agreeable to us that the Salvation Army workers distribute the Scripture. The League was happy to comply. The Bibles were sent to the city and subsequently placed in the homes of those people who lost all of their possessions.

AN ENTIRE CITY IS REACHED (APRIL 1945)

The Grand Rapids Ministers' Association accepted the offer of the American Home Bible League to furnish Bibles for all the Bibleless homes in the city. The Rev. Jerry Veldman had conducted a similar campaign in Kalamazoo a few years before and was appointed the General Chairman for the committee. Representatives from eleven different denominations and some ninety churches volunteered for the canvass.

A community chest map was obtained. On this map the city was divided into thirty-five districts. Captains were appointed to take charge of these districts and different blocks in the city thus were assigned.

A letter sent to all the ministers explained the program and gave general suggestions concerning the work. An announcement was also included that Mr. Chapman would be in the city during the week of March 5. A schedule of

41

programs was published and churches were urged to invite their people to attend the presentations in their community. They were also encouraged to make use of Mr. Chapman's presence in the city at special meetings.

Sometime later a glowing report on Bible distribution in Grand Rapids was sent to us:

"Under the auspices of the Grand Rapids Ministerial Association the city of Grand Rapids was "Bibleized" recently. The American Home Bible League of Chicago furnished the necessary Bibles. Four months were taken to set up the program, ninety churches registered to help in the work, and 1,518 people volunteered to stop at every home in the city. At the instruction meeting, Central Reformed Church was completely filled with workers and Messrs. Chapman and Evers of the League addressed the group. In the course of the week 28,000 calls were made and approximately 1,200 Bibles placed. Bibles were placed in homes where there were no Bibles. Each family who received the gift Bible promised that the Book would be read. Over one hundred homes requesting Bibles, according to the cards, belonged to the Roman Catholic church."

Rev. Peter G. Holwerda

SOWING IN THE SWAMPLAND

When Cuba was still open to the gospel the League's ambitious program of distribution was centered in the Province of Matanzas and in the town of Jaguey Grande. Thousands of copies of the Scripture were sent throughout the island.

During this time a railroad ran from a town called Australia near our office in Cuba, to the southern coast of the island. The area through which this railroad ran was called the "Seneca" or swampland. This was the area of Cuba that received international publicity when troops representing the counter-revolution landed in Castro's

Cuba in the Bay of Pigs fiasco of 1961.

In the company of a few missionaries we decided to investigate the stories we had heard about this swampland. It was reported that 3,000 people lived there. There were no policemen, no roads, no schools, no hospitals, no deliveries, just 3,000 people at the end of a railraod track. A missionary or two had visited the area, but none had been there for any length of time. We rented a little train for eleven dollars a day and began our strange journey. The tracks were crooked; in some places the ties were under water; in others the rails disappeared. But finally we came to the swampland.

We began to call on homes and distribute the Scripture and we had some wonderful experiences. We came to one hut in which a woman anxiously awaited us. She had noticed our arrival at the little village and welcomed us. The missionary asked her if she had ever read a New Testatment. Much to our surprise she answered, "Yes." The missionary asked her where she got the Testament.

She replied, "A relative brought it from a distant town."

The missionary asked if he could see it. How our hearts jumped with joy when she came out with the familiar red Testament printed by the League. The missionary asked, "Do you read the Testament?"

She answered, "I read it every night." This woman had never gone to church, nor had she ever heard a missionary or a pastor preach.

Why did the missionary then ask her the question, "Do you think the Lord Jesus Christ is coming back again?" How could she know.

But the moment he asked the question a broad, almost toothless grin, broke on her face. She jabbed her finger up toward the sky and pointed at a big puffy white cloud that

43

was floating by and exclaimed in excited tones, "Yes, He is coming again. He is coming again. He is going to be coming on the clouds in the sky."

In sharp contrast to this experience, much later in the day, almost at the time when we were ready to leave, we called on another home.

The missionary asked the question, "Do you have a Testament in your home?"

The woman replied, "What is a Testament?"

Quite taken aback the missionary said, "It is part of the Bible." The old lady then asked, "What is a Bible?"

The missionary said, "It is a Book that God gave, it talks about Jesus Christ."

The woman seemed to be in deep thought and then she said, "Yes, I heard that name before."

"Where did you hear it?" he asked.

"Well," she said, "my husband attended a funeral in the town of Australia and after it was over he went into a saloon. There were some men drinking there and I remember his telling me that one of them kept repeating that name over and over again."

As we were about to leave the swampland we noticed a sign. It said, "Coca-Cola 5c." Here were 3,000 people living at the end of a railroad track a little over 100 miles away from the greatest Christian nation the world has ever known. They knew all about our Coca-Cola but .this woman had only heard of Jesus Christ through the cursing of a tourist.

HOMES IN HOLLAND, MICHIGAN, CANVASSED
(APRIL 1945)

What laymen can do once they have caught the enthusiasm, the inspiration and vision of a task and when a tangible program has been handed them, was demonstrated in a big way in Holland on the Sunday afternoon following

Easter. The program was a city-wide religious survey, the primary purpose of which was to get data on the unchurched family situation in Holland and environs and to place Bibles, provided by the American Home Bible League, in Bibleless homes. The manpower for this task included some 200 men drawn from every church of every denomination in Holland. A marvelous spirit of Christian unity and solidarity came to expression in the willing cooperation of these men in carrying out their assigned tasks. The groundwork and plans for this canvass were laid by a committee representing the Holland Ministerial Association where this project originated, plus delegates from the Holland Federation of Men's Bible Classes. Every church was tapped for helpers and every church responded. This seemingly great job of canvassing a city of some 18,000 population was accomplished for the large part in a few hours on a single Sunday afternoon. Systematic zoning and districting of the city with teams assigned to particular areas made the work a success at a minimum expenditure of time and effort.

The survey itself was simple. The men were not asked to evangelize the homes but merely to get the facts about the church relationships of each family by way of questions on the card provided by the League. The evangelistic work by the various local churches followed up the survey once the facts were in and all the unchurched families catalogued. Tabulations on the basis of cards returned indicated there were approximately 4,000 families contacted of which about 500 were without church connections. Some 100 Bibles were left in homes. That religious picture of the so-called "churchy" city of Holland was not as bright as most of us in our town thought. Holland, as the proverb goes, with a church on almost every corner still has within its bosom many who

45

are not yet brought under the gospel of Jesus Christ or affiliated with a church where that gospel is radiated. What must the situation be in other localities not as well favored? Here is a lasting challenge for the church of Christ to bring the Word of God to those not yet in the faith and for every member to be a witness for Him. We pray that as the religious picture of our city has been unveiled through this survey the church here will show the passion for souls and sense its calling to reach out for those still outside.

The clergy of Holland deeply appreciates the fine Christian spirit of interest and helpfulness in this work rendered by Mr. Chapman and the assistance of the American Home Bible League in providing the Bibles for this canvass. May God richly bless the consecrated program of the League.

Rev. Lawrence Veltkamp

EVEN THE HILLS OF KENTUCKY WERE REACHED (1945)

This is the story of how the Word of God came to the hills of Jackson County, Kentucky, in a new and wonderful way. Through the sponsorship of the American Home Bible League, the staff of the Reformed Church in America Mission, together with many of the mountain people have "Bibleized" this county.

At a meeting of the ministers of the staff the mechanics of the program were determined and set in motion. A previous visitation of Mr. Chapman, Mr. Vander Meer, and the Rev. John A. Klaaren helped greatly to prepare for the program. The names of the families were secured from the County Ration Board and all the names were placed on individual religious survey cards, specially prepared and printed for this work. The work of informing the people was then begun and word went out to all the county concerning the coming campaign. The school districts and our Sunday school, as well as the larger population area, were listed as distribution centers and then leaders and workers were chosen to do the work.

From schools, Sunday schools, homes, churches, groups went on foot, on mules and horses, and in cars to bring the Word of God to those who did not have the Truth. As a result 2,000 families were visited by 100 workers and 650 Bibles were placed.

The results are becoming more interesting than was the original distribution. A teacher has asked for a Bible for a new family which has just moved into the neighborhood. An indifferent man has faithfully attended special services, took part in one of the meetings and is manifesting keen interest in the things of God. Evangelistic services were held in one center by request, and a Sunday school has been organized. In many areas the Thanksgiving-to-Christmas Bible reading program was followed through. Without these Bibles this would have been impossible.

Raymond B. Drukker

As the Lord moved in the hearts of His people in such areas as Paterson and New Brunswick, New Jersey; Danforth, Illinois; Fond du Lac, Wisconsin; Pella, Iowa; and other cities across the United States, and as homes were called upon and the Scripture left, many enthusiastic endorsements of pastors, missionaries and other Christian workers were received.

BIBLE DISTRIBUTION EXPERIENCES

ON A CRUISE SHIP

Some years ago my wife and I went on an escorted tour to Alaska. There were about eighty others in this group and we had a wonderful time of Christian fellowship.

Each time the cruise ship docked between Seattle and Alaska, I left the vessel and contacted the local pastors. A number of tour members became inquisitive and after learning what I was doing, joined me in making these calls. We discovered that there were quite a few pastors who seemed interested in reaching their community. As a result, several shipments of Scriptures were made to them.

One evening, Dr. Louis Benes, editor of the *Church Herald*, a denominational publication of the Reformed Church in America, and tour conductor, asked me to present the work of the World Home Bible League. This invitation was accepted and as a result we received many thousands of dollars sent in by fellow tour members in the years that followed. Some of the people we first met on this tour are still contributing. One of our fellow travelers now serves as a member of our international board.

We are grateful to God for the opportunity of being able to go on this tour to Alaska. It opened many doors for us. We also met many interested pastors enroute. What a thrill it is to look back and see how God lays burdens for reaching the lost and how He can use us in many different circumstances in life. Yes, sometimes even during a vacation cruise.

IN A CAB

During World War II it was my privilege to be invited to address a group of pastors in Milwaukee, Wisconsin. My wife joined me. We went by train and took a taxicab from the station. It proved to be an old dilapidated cab that evidently had not been replaced because new equipment was not available due to the war. I was quite surprised that such poor equipment would be permitted on the streets for public use.

We were going up a hill when the motor began to knock and hammer. I wasn't too sure we were going to make it. I asked the driver, "What's the matter with this thing?"

He answered, "I think there is a bearing going to hell."

I commented, "That wouldn't be as serious as if you should go there."

He replied, "I never thought of that."

There are millions of people today who never think in terms of eternity. Even though they do not think of it, it is still the truth. Millions are on their way to a Christless eternity. These people do not feel their need of Christ, but we know that it is only through Him that man can be saved. This is the paramount reason why the World Home Bible League is dedicated to the distribution of God's Word. We know from experience that the printed page is a mighty effective way of pointing men and women away from eternal destruction to the road that leads to heaven and happiness.

The cab driver accepted a Bible on the promise that he would read it. Then he asked, "Are you a preacher?"

I told him I was only a layman. It is the responsibility of each of us, isn't it, to bring a Christian witness to those with whom we come in contact, and God can use laymen, male or female, in the important task of telling others about the love of Christ.

49

DURING A FERRY RIDE

I was on the Staten Island ferry which leaves from South Ferry adjacent to Battery Park and goes to Staten Island. I was to address one of the oldest Bible classes in the country, the Men's Sunday Bible Class of Staten Island. A very dear friend of mine from Paterson, New Jersey, accompanied me. As we stood together looking around at the scenery we noticed a man drawing sketches of people on the ferry boat. He appeared to be very talented. I walked over to him, reached out my hand, and remarked, "Congratulations, you certainly have tremendous talent." He was pleased by the compliment.

"By the way, I have in mind to ask a number of people today a very personal question. It is so personal that perhaps you might be reluctant to answer," I said.

He shrugged his shoulders and in a matter-of-fact way said, "Go ahead, ask me anything you want."

I asked, "What does Jesus Christ mean to you?"

Somewhat taken aback, he floundered for a moment. "Jesus? Let me see," he stumbled and faltered. He didn't have an answer.

Then I observed, "You don't acknowledge Him as the Son of God, or as the Lord of your life? Are you familiar with the Scripture?"

He confessed, "No, I am not. I never had a copy of the Scripture."

I offered to give him a Gospel of John. "Would you promise to read it?" I asked. He agreed to. "Would you like to know why God wrote this Bible?" I asked.

I urged him to read John 20:31. He complied, and I concluded, "That is why God wrote it. He wrote it that you might believe that Jesus is the Christ, the Son of God, and that believing, you might have life through His name. Listen, friend, if you accept the Christ of this Book, and if you put your faith in Him, you and I will some day be in heaven together."

As we were getting off the ferry some moments later he tapped me on the shoulder and thanked me for talking to him. "I needed something like this," he said, and departed.

ENCOUNTER WITH A PRIEST

One day while driving in Chicago I stopped to pick up a Catholic priest who signaled for a ride. Along the way the conversation focused on our ministry. He told me that he knew of the work and that it involved Bible distribution.

Although the introduction was quite uneventful and the first few moments were rather pleasant, we began to clash very sharply on a number of things we discussed. Finally, stopping my car and taking a Bible out of the trunk, I parked alongside the road. Together we discussed rather heatedly the Bible and its teachings until nearly noon. When he eventually stepped out of the car he had a copy of the King James Bible under his arm. Something compelled me to grab him by the shoulder as he was leaving and I said, "Let's pray." I prayed for him and asked that the Holy Spirit might speak to his heart and enlighten it.

Two years later a letter came from him. He was now a priest in Iowa, and he wrote that he was coming to Chicago and wanted to meet me.

In due time he arrived at my office and one of the first things he said was, "So you are a businessman. I have often wondered how anyone in the business world could talk to me the way you did the last time. Where did you get your theological training to talk to me in that manner?"

I replied, "From between the covers of the book that I gave you and which you often deny to your laity and many times don't believe in yourself. I am thankful to God that the laity do have the Scripture today and that organizations such as ours distribute many Bibles to your people."

Some weeks later the following letter was received from him: "I am ready to start a new life in the ministry of Jesus Christ and I have seen the light. With millions of others I was misguided through tunnels of darkness, blind obedience, fear and trembling, which Christ came to dispel and to destroy. I hope and pray that for Christ's sake I will be able to make a new start in life immediately."

HARRY AND THE BIBLE

Our family went to look over a summer home on a lake south of the city of Chicago. As we glanced over the property we could not help hearing the rather abusive language being used by the people on the adjoining property. Our first reaction was that it certainly would not be nice to live next door to such people. Our second thought was that perhaps we could be an influence on them.

We bought the property. One afternoon we were working in the yard and our neighbor was in his. A conversation developed, carried on over the fence. It was concluded with his invitation, "Why don't you come over tonight?" Just then my wife came out of the house. She was asked and she agreed.

At his home that evening he turned to me and said, "You know, you are quite a strange fellow. You have a real nice home, you have a good boat, but I don't see you around on Sunday and very seldom during the week. I just don't understand it."

I explained, "Having a summer place like this is a very great blessing, but there are also other goals in life. My real interest is something else that takes everything that I can put into it. Having a place like this often presents a temptation to take time that could otherwise be put into

52

the work that lies close to my heart."

His curiosity was aroused, "What kind of interest are you talking about?"

I replied, "We distribute Bibles all over the world."

Seizing the opportunity, I tried to follow through. "By the way, wouldn't it be foolish to distribute Bibles all over the world and then not offer one to my next-door neighbor? That wouldn't be neighborly, would it?"

At this point his wife replied, rather defiantly, "I am a Catholic and my sons are altar boys."

We told her that this was fine and that many of our good friends are Catholics.

Her husband had been listening to the conversation and then in a sort of matter-of-fact tone said, "But I am nothing at all."

His statement revealed that he had very little spiritual depth, if any. Later he informed us that he had a very responsible position with one of the largest labor unions in Chicago. The man admitted that he was nothing. That's a perfect place to begin.

Looking him in the eye, I said, "Harry, I have often had to talk with people a long time before they would admit what you just did, that you are nothing." I continued by telling him that we must begin at that point and that we in ourselves are nothing. It is then that Christ can do the most effective work in our lives.

The conversation then drifted into a lighter vein. There was much laughter about many things. When we were about to leave, I went to the car and said, "Here, neighbor, is a copy of the Bible we offer all over the world, but we should have a promise from you that you will read it." The wife readily replied that she was willing to promise. The husband added his promise too, but not quite so enthusiastically.

Three weeks later, much to my surprise, my neighbor called me over and asked whether he might have a dozen more Bibles. Although very curious, I complied with the request. A month later we met again. He asked, "Do you know what I did with those Bibles? I gave them to some of my associates who are leaders in different unions. I presented them at a convention held in a well-known hotel and I received several letters expressing appreciation for the Bibles." He then gave me a contribution of forty dollars.

Deeply moved, I said, "By the way, I am certain that you realize that in making this gift you are expressing a desire to tell others about Jesus Christ."

He replied with some reservation, "Yeah, I suppose so."

Reaching out across the fence, I said, "Congratulations to you."

He asked me, "What are you congratulating me for?"

I told him because he was a missionary. He exclaimed, "Well, I'll be -" Then catching himself just in time he added, "I never thought things would come to that."

In the months that followed this man encountered extreme difficulties. He became seriously ill and spent much time in and out of hospitals. Finally, they sent him to Mayo Clinic. There his ailment was diagnosed as possibly terminal.

One day his wife met me and said, "No one has ever been able to talk about spiritual things to my husband but he appreciates talking to you. Please keep it up."

Harry was not feeling very well the next time we met. We prayed together, and later Betty and I left on a tour to Australia, so it was some time before we met again.

Harry's physical condition had not improved. Among other things, he admitted that he was not feeling too well and that he had made up his mind to join the Catholic

Church. "What is your opinion about this?" he asked.

Leaning toward the chair in which he was sitting, I expressed myself in this way: "Harry, we have been very frank with each other in times past and I trust that we shall continue to be. The most important thing in the whole world is that you believe in the Lord Jesus Christ. If you look to Calvary for remission of your sins, and your faith is not in your church, not in your priest, nor in any pastor, then go with your wife to the Catholic Church. But, whatever you do, look to Jesus and Him only for your salvation."

Later on we discovered that a Catholic priest came in to see Harry five times a week and read the Bible that we had given. Our friend died some time later and at the funeral we were told that the presence of this Bible in his home and the subsequent testimony had a profound effect upon his life.

AS YOU TRAVEL ASK US

Together with a pastor and his wife, we stopped at a gas station. There we noticed the very familiar sign, "As You Travel Ask Us." Explaining to my pastor friend that I wanted to leave a witness with the attendant, I ordered gas and then commented, "Many travelers are attracted by that sign, 'As You Travel Ask Us.' You certainly must have many interesting questions asked of you."

He assured me, "Almost every question under the sun."

I probed, "Did anybody ever ask how to get to heaven?"

His brow wrinkled and he appeared taken aback, then slowly he answered, "No-o."

"Suppose someone came in here and asked, 'Mister, how do you get to heaven?' Could you tell him how to get there? What would your answer be?"

He replied hesitatingly, "Well, I really don't know what

I would tell him."

I placed a Gospel of John in his hand and explained to him that all of us are travelers on life's highway and that in many ways the Gospel of John is a map, and we would be willing to give him a copy of this map if he were willing to study it. He replied that he would do so.

Before we parted, John 20:31 was pointed out to him. We asked him to read it. He stood close to the window of the car and read the verse, "But these are written, that ye might believe that Jesus is the Christ, the Son of God; and that believing ye might have life through his name."

I added, "That is exactly why God wrote the Book, young man, and that is why we want to give it to you."

His answer surprised us. "You know, I am not the happiest man on earth. Thanks for talking to me. This may be just what I need."

A "TOUGH CUSTOMER"

A group of young people were canvassing in a certain section of Chicago that was considered one of the more difficult areas. I was assisting in this canvass and after climbing several flights of stairs, I came to an apartment and knocked on the door. For a moment I did not think anyone was at home. Then suddenly the door was thrown open so violently it seemed as though it was going off its hinges. A gruff man on the other side of the door asked, "What do you want?"

I told him why I had come and concluded by offering him a Bible if he did not have one.

He looked at me with anger in his eyes, "We don't have any time for that kind of stuff," and with that he slammed the door in my face.

With a prayer in my heart, I knocked on the door again. Once again it was opened abruptly. "You still here?" he asked.

"Yes," I replied, "You don't seem to be too interested in spiritual things. Frankly, I am a lot more interested in your wife and in your kiddies than I am in you. Did you see the article in the newspaper last night about the youth problems we are having in our country?" He said he did. I continued, "We have a bigger problem than you know about. One that is a lot more serious. It is a parent problem."

He looked at me for a moment and then his anger seemed to leave him. He invited me to come into his home. As soon as someone displayed love and concern for him and his family he became interested. In fact, he accepted a Bible and the children were enrolled in the Sunday school.

SOWING AND REAPING

One day a pastor observed the delivery of more than twenty tons of Scriptures to our League office. He remarked, "Say, wouldn't it be wonderful if every one of those Bibles could be used to bring a person to a saving knowledge of Christ?" I turned to him and replied, "Yes, that would be wonderful, and wouldn't it be wonderful if everyone you preached to during the thirty years of your ministry would come to a saving knowledge of Christ?"

We know that wherever the Scripture is distributed it will accomplish the purpose of God. We know that it cannot and will not return unto God void. But we also know that in any warfare, whether it be spiritual or carnal, some ammunition is always lost in the battle.

The Bible is compared to precious seed, and in Mark 4 we read the parable of the sower. Once again, the truth of the Scripture is apparent. Some seed falls on the ground and it is scorched, some seed falls on stony ground, and some is choked by the weeds, but how we thank God for the seed that brings forth one hundredfold. It is our task to sow the seed, but it is God who gives the increase. We are thrilled with reports of many souls saved in many lands. If only one soul were saved through Bible distribution, how wonderful that would be, for we are told time and time again that one soul is worth more than all the wealth of this world. We would be willing to settle for that, but God has humbled us by giving us many souls for our hire.

OUR SEED IS THE WORD
AND THE FIELD IS THE WORLD

God had given us a tiny acorn. The acorn had sprouted into life and had become a tree. As the days wore on into months and years this little tree was to become a mighty oak and its branches would reach into areas beyond our fondest expectation.

As sowers went out to sow, others became interested in the project. Before we knew it men and women all over the United States and Canada and in many parts of the world became involved in our program. The men and women sowers of the Word represented many cultural backgrounds and many denominations. All were possessed with one driving passion: to get the Word of God in written form into the hands of men and women wherever they were. Here are a few of their encouraging letters to us.

ALASKA

My husband and I are missionaries among Russian people here in Alaska. We can appreciate the need of the Word of God. The need for that Word on the Island of Afognak is truly great. We need 50 to 100 Bibles, but lack funds to make such Bibles available. We are missionaries under the Slovak Gospel Association supported by the First Reformed Church of Mt. Greenwood.

Mr. and Mrs. Pederson

JAPAN

The executive secretary of the Lutheran Board of Foreign Missions wrote: "We know that you have supplied many copies of the Scriptures for distribution to people who have written in after they have heard the Lutheran Hour and enrolled in our Bible correspondence courses. One of the most potent forces for the establishment of the Christian church in Japan is the dissemination of the Bible. Your contributions of Bibles is very much appreciated."

FROM THE HEART OF NIGERIA

A perspiring male runner entered our large compound. In his hand was a pleasant surprise for the village natives; the first shipment of 200 copies of *God Speaks* in the Tiv language had arrived. It was the first of many additional weekly allotments to come across the trails from sixty miles away. Missionaries and natives were jubilant and within a short while the entire consignment was distributed.

The translation of *God Speaks* in the Tiv language was completed under the direction of the Rev. Rits Tadema in cooperation with missionaries of the Sudan United Mission.

SOUTHERN INDIA

We have received Tamil Bibles and New Testaments. Through the assistance which you have given us these Bibles and New Testaments were given to village people who have no Bible. We live in a village center where there are people all around us who have never heard the Word of God. As our gospel workers go among these people they take the Bibles and New Testaments you provided. Through your help the Bible has come as a light to many a darkened home where there is nothing else to lead the people to God. A number of souls have been won through the reading of the Word. May I express appreciation for this fine way of helping missionaries distribute the Word of God in India.

Mrs. Robert Edwards

Tamil District, South Indian Assemblies of God

LIBERIA

The Prospect Street Christian Reformed Church sent a shipment of the Scriptures to Liberia through the World Home Bible League. These copies were donated to a missionary who conducted the funeral service for an airline pilot who perished in a crash of a commercial airliner in Liberia.

PUERTO RICO

There has been a very interesting response to Scriptures offered in the Spanish tongue to students here at the Inter-American University of Puerto Rico. *God Speaks,* the Gospel of John, and the New Testament have received a brisk interest. We are grateful for the wonderful things which you have done to help us minister here. Puerto Rico seems to be hungry for knowledge, and above all for a faith that will stand up in our present world.

KOWLOON, HONG KONG

Thousands of World Home Bible League Bibles were distributed through the Rev. John Bechtel of the Servicemen's Christian Fellowship in Kowloon. These Testaments were carried by English servicemen to their homeland. Other servicemen from the United States and other nations also received copies of the free Bibles. One English serviceman was converted and has since become a minister of the gospel.

COLOMBIA

Rev. Elof H. Anderson, missionary to Colombia, South America, under The Evangelical Alliance Mission, conducted a campaign in which he placed 10,000 copies of the Spanish version of *God Speaks* in the town of Cucuta,

Colombia. *God Speaks* is a small booklet of selected Scripture portions.

LATIN AMERICA

Burdened for the people of Latin America, Professor David Vila and students of the Reformed Bible Institute sent more than 12,000 copies of the Scripture to Spanish-speaking people in Mexico, Guatemala, Honduras, El Salvador, Dominican Republic, Venezuela, Colombia, Peru, Bolivia, Chile, Argentina, and Uruguay.

HAWAII

This summer I had the opportunity to distribute thousands of portions of God's Word provided through the World Home Bible League. There are still thousands here who are worshiping idols and many others who have forsaken visible idols and turned to the idols of materialism. I cannot thank you enough for your kindness in helping me with literature for Hawaii. This fall I plan to go to Europe with twenty other students to distribute God's Word in France, Germany, Belgium, Holland, and Austria.

Tom Maynard

MIAMI, FLORIDA

The city of Miami is well known for its resort attractions. There are many of Jewish extraction among the millions of people who congregate there. A missionary who worked among these winter visitors reported, "There are many here in Miami, the tourist mecca of the world, who are interested in Christianity and who ask for Bibles. Many Jewish people are among those who ask. They want to look up the prophecies and their fulfillment concerning the Messiah. Sometimes I can barely keep up with the requests. In one campaign alone I gave out thousands of New Testaments to Jewish people in Miami.

"The other day on one of the main thoroughfares of

Miami I did some street witnessing. I had a large sign which announced that I would give a free New Testament to any Jew who would promise to read it. Many Jewish people came up and requested a copy. I believe that this is God's hour for reaching the Jews. Never before have I seen them so receptive to the Holy Scriptures."

Let us pray for this brother as he attempts to reach God's promised people with the Holy Scriptures. He is one of the hosts of faithful sowers who work throughout this wide world of ours.

AN OLD MAN'S PLEDGE

Dr. John Piet, who was formerly one of our directors in India, introduced us to an old man who lived in Madras whose name was John Maxwell. Old Mr. Maxwell left England with a promise to the Lord that he would distribute at least 100,000 copies of the Scripture to 100,000 people in India. Mr. Maxwell lived as an Indian and sacrificed all the conveniences he formerly enjoyed. His living quarters consisted of one room with a cot and a little wooden table and chair. With zeal and diligence he set about his task of reaching 100,000 people. When Mr. Maxwell approached Dr. Piet the first time, Dr. Piet hesitated to give him any material, but the more he got to know John Maxwell the more he recognized his genuine sincerity. Here was a man who had a deep concern to reach the lost for Christ. It seemed that John Maxwell, living in poverty, worked every waking hour. Some years passed after we first met this elderly saint and heard of his project. We often wondered whether he had ever reached his goal or whether he had given up. The goal had seemed quite impossible to achieve.

Then one day we received a strange letter. It came from an unknown address in Bangkok, Thailand, from our old friend John Maxwell. He wrote, "I have fulfilled my pledge

63

to the Lord. He has been very good to me. I have placed 100,000 of your Scriptures among 100,000 people in India and now I am going to place 100,000 Scriptures among the people in Thailand. Will you help me?"

GOD SPEAKS PRINTED IN INDONESIA

The Rev. Spencer De Jong, the League's first international director, recently served World Vision in Indonesia as its acting director.

While there he was appalled at the few copies of Scripture available for distribution among the people. He wrote to the World Home Bible League, requesting that the League consider the translation and publication of its Scripture booklet, *God Speaks,* in the Indonesian language. The project was approved.

The Bible Society of Indonesia was solicited and help was graciously given. In the first printing, the League released 100,000 copies of *God Speaks,* 50,000 of them to be distributed through the World Vision office at Malang. Some copies of Scripture will be distributed to children attending Bible schools. Fifty thousand will be used throughout the island in evangelistic campaigns sponsored by the evangelist John Haggai. Churches will give them out in their communities. The Emmanuel Presbyterian Church in Djakarta, which is one of the oldest on the island and was built in the year 1600, will be one of the participating churches in the coming distribution. Other copies of the Scripture will be distributed through laymen, among them Mr. Tan Ik Sang, who has a ministry at the harbor. It is also expected that a number of copies will be shipped to Borneo.

JAPAN

General Douglas MacArthur wrote:

"I have read with great interest the plan of the World Home Bible League to engage in Bible distribution in

Japan. I have many times publicly stated my beliefs that Christianity through the sacred Scriptures offers to the Japanese people a sure and stable foundation on which to build a democratic nation and have expressed the hope that the Bible can be placed in the home of every family in Japan.

"It gives me great pleasure to commend the plan of the Japan Home Bible League to introduce the Bible to non-Christian homes through personal contacts made by the laity. I trust that this evangelistic effort will meet with success. The sponsorship of the World Home Bible League in this activity is greatly appreciated. You may quote parts of or all of this letter if it will give encouragement to your worthy movement."

Sincerely yours,

(Signed) General Douglas MacArthur

Shortly after the receipt of this letter the World Home Bible League Board voted to begin its first foreign distribution and to create its first foreign affiliate. An office was rented in the Bible House in Tokyo, and the original commitment was to place 100,000 Testaments in 100,000 Japanese homes. Again we felt our weakness, and again we cried to God to undertake for us. When a gift was received at the World Home Bible League office for one thousand dollars designated for Japan, we felt once again that God was encouraging us. This came at a time when we were not receiving many contributions of this size and, because it was earmarked for Japan when we had given the project so little publicity, it was deeply appreciated and proved to be an inspiration to us in our work.

Since that time hundreds of thousands of copies of Scripture have been placed in Japan through missionaries representing a cross section of all the religious life in Japan. Japanese Testaments were placed in hospitals and in mining camps. Many of them were distributed to fishermen, and a great number were given to students who were anxiously inquiring into the Christian faith. An advertisement placed in some of the larger newspapers in Tokyo also brought in many requests. Bible correspondence courses were released using our New Testament as a textbook.

In the year marking the twentieth anniversary of the founding of the World Home Bible League, it was my privilege to visit Japan with my wife and Mr. C. L. Evers, Sr., and his wife. Upon arrival in Tokyo I was given a certificate. It was written in both Japanese and English, and said: "In this memorable year when the twentieth anniversary of the founding of the World Home Bible League was celebrated and the 200,000th placement of the Japanese New Testament in homes of Japan was commemorated, we, on this happy occasion, welcome to this country the party headed by Mr. William A. Chapman. This certificate is presented to Mr. William A. Chapman, faithful servant of God, in gratitude and appreciation of his untiring efforts in building the Kingdom of God and in prayer in the name of our Lord of his ever long and continuous efforts to evangelize the whole world."

This was signed by Mr. Shun Suzuki, president of the Japan Home Bible League, Senji Tsuru, director, Mr. Kojiro Hata, its treasurer, and the secretary of the Japan Home Bible League, Masasuke Masutomi.

BIBLE VAN

In several parts of the world, particularly in Spain and India, the World Home Bible League Scripture distribution was done through the use of Bible vans. A good example of this is Spain, where a truck was purchased by a missionary organization and many of the Bibles and Testaments were supplied by the World Home Bible

League. This Bible van went into various villages to meet the people where they lived; tens of thousands of copies of Scripture were distributed in this manner.

MOTOR BIKE

Our Testaments were even distributed by motor bike in Ceylon. An evangelist of the Dutch Reformed Church visited more than forty villages. The saddlebags on his bike were loaded with copies of Scripture in the Sinhalese tongue to reach men and women in Ceylon with the printed Word.

NEWSPAPER EVANGELISM

A veteran missionary, Dr. Albertus Pieters, began a very interesting ministry in Japan called "newspaper evangelism." Added to the evangelistic message in the newspaper was an invitation to the readers to write in for copies of the Scripture. This work continued even after Dr. Pieters died, and the World Home Bible League supplied many of the Testaments used in this evangelistic effort.

It was our privilege some years later to be at the Reformed Bible Institute in Grand Rapids, Michigan, where we met a man from Japan who had been a former steelworker. He had answered an advertisement in a Tokyo newspaper. He received one of our Testaments, read it, and became a Christian. Now he was preparing for a life of Christian service!

Copies of the Scripture provided by the League have also been used in newspaper evangelism throughout the U.S.A. and other countries.

AIRMAIL FROM GOD

Some years ago, about 1952, the founder of the Airmail from God Mission in Mexico, Rev. Nyles Huffman, came to the World Home Bible League's office. He told how God had directed him to take a small airplane and fly over unmapped areas of Mexico. There he sowed the gospel by airdropping little Gospels of John through a chute in the bottom of the plane. He went back to these villages later with an evangelist to help explain the Scripture.

The World Home Bible League did not supply the gospels that were dropped from the airplane but they did supply thousands of New Testaments that were used in the follow-up work.

Nyles Huffman met his death flying a plane to bring the gospel to the lost in Mexico. For many years a few Gospels of John, stained with the blood of Nyles Huffman, were in a file at the Airmail from God Mission offices in Mexico. The great work that he founded continues and now by special arrangement with the Airmail from God ministry, the World Home Bible League prints, at subsidized cost, many of the little gospels that are today flown into remote areas of Mexico, and South and Central America.

FOOD FOR THE SOUL

Some years ago we were invited to Celeryville, Ohio. Many copies of Scripture have been distributed in that area. A grocery man seemed to be one of the persons who was most interested in the distribution. He had a supermarket filled with the usual groceries one would expect to find in such a store.

One shelf in the store was set aside for Bibles and he had a little sign made up, "Do you have a Bible in your home?" He offered to give a Bible upon the promise that it would be read. He also had other Scripture material.

In Grand Rapids, another grocer who owned a supermarket devoted several shelves to Christian literature such as that produced by Moody Bible Institute, and a special section for World Home Bible League Bibles, Testaments, and Scripture portions. These men were offering food for the soul as they sold food for the body.

BLESSED CHRISTMAS

A group of youngsters representing a South Holland church approached one of our board members who was in the landscaping business and sold Christmas trees. They had a novel idea for spreading the Christmas joy. After the board member heard the story he agreed.

Each person who bought a Christmas tree from this man found neatly attached to one of its branches a little Christmas booklet published by the World Home Bible League entitled, "A Message for you on Christmas."

SHANTYMEN

Canadian Christians are familiar with a wonderful missionary organization called the Shantymen's Mission. Its missionaries are men committed to bringing the Word to remote areas of Canada, including lumber camps, mining villages, etc.

The Shantymen's Mission has used many copies of the World Home Bible League Scripture. One time it was our privilege to be aboard its boat. We went along the rugged Vancouver coastline visiting lighthouse keepers, a group of Japanese who were oyster fishing, a turkey farm, and lumber camps. Everywhere we went copies of the World Home Bible League Scripture were distributed.

IMMIGRATION

Years ago Canada experienced a tremendous immigration of families from the Netherlands. The World Home Bible League provided several thousand Bibles, which were given to these immigrants as they stepped off the boat. The Bibles were in their new adopted language, English, and many began to learn this new tongue through the reading of Holy Scripture.

MIGRATORY WORKERS

Very early in our ministry the migrant worker became the object of Bible distribution. Spanish Testaments were first distributed in the Borculo area of Michigan among the Mexican migrants who picked cucumbers. These Testaments were also distributed among those who picked cherries in Michigan and the workers who harvested celery near Willard, Ohio, were also given thousands of World Home Bible League Testaments. In California, migratory grape pickers were also reached with the Gospel. In Minnesota, churches used our Testaments to provide the migrant worker with the Word.

Many interesting incidents occurred during these distribution projects. The zeal of those who did the sowing was encouraging. One man who worked in the Lansing, Michigan, area had a novel way of reaching migrants. He would come to a camp on Sunday afternoon and ask for permission to preach. When permission was given he would get the men together and then he would ask, "Who is the most honest, reliable man among you? Who is the man who will not lie?" There would be considerable laughter and finally, after some jesting, they would pick one man. The missionary would ask him to come up front and then ask, "Can you read? You can? Well, that is fine. What does it say on the front of this large Bible that I hold?"

The man would read loud enough for all to hear that it was a Roman Catholic Bible, approved by the Pope in Rome for reading. Then the missionary would distribute the little red Testaments to each of the men and ask them to turn to a certain page. He would then encourage the man who had been chosen by them to read in the Catholic Bible the same passage that appeared in the little red Testaments. He would lead them in many Scripture-reading exercises and then he would ask them if there were any difference between the authorized Catholic Bible and the Testament. They would answer no.

Through this method he brought the Gospel effectively

to many of these people who never before heard the real story of Jesus and His love. One day when I visited him he went through this particular procedure and then he gave the migrant workers an opportunity to "take a personal stand for Jesus Christ." Every man present came forward!

REFUGEES

For many years the World Home Bible League had an effective Scripture distribution program among Cubans. It was a very extensive distribution, but it ended abruptly in 1962 when Fidel Castro seized a large number of Testaments that had been sent to Cuba. From that day on only a few World Home Bible League Testaments filtered through Castro's red curtain.

Then the refugees began to arrive in Miami! Thousands of them were air lifted and churches began to minister to their needs. The League supplied tens of thousands of New Testaments and Scripture portions. Some of these were given to Christian families who had lost everything in Cuba. Other portions and New Testaments were given to non-Christian families. Some copies of Scripture were inserted in packets of food and bundles of clothing. Many of the pastors working with the World Home Bible League in Cuba also became involved in distribution in their new ministry among Cuban refugees.

SOWING BESIDE ALL WATERS

Down in Tampico, Mexico, Mr. Abe Marcus worked for many years on the Tamesi River. Mr. Marcus would take his boat and travel far inland stopping along the way to visit families. Many of these people had no way of getting to civilization. They lived along the river all their lives and supplies were brought to them by boat. There was even a beer boat that brought beer up the river. Most of the people along the river were farmers. All of them were among the poorest of the poor.

On each trip the "mission boat" made, copies of the Spanish New Testaments, *God Speaks,* and Scripture cards were part of the cargo, along with the aspirin tablets and vitamins, and sometimes pieces of clothing for the children. Copies of the Scripture were distributed to all who would receive them and who could read. Several outstanding conversions resulted from this distribution and these are reported in another part of this book.

EXPO 1967

The Canadian Home Bible League, under the direction of Mr. John Vander Boom, participated in a religious exhibit at the Canadian Exposition during 1967-68. It was called the "Sermons from Science Pavilion." This was a special project sponsored by a group of Christian businessmen supported through evangelical churches. Although it had no official connection with the Moody Bible Institute, it made use of that organization's well-known "Sermons from Science" films. After the regular .film had been shown, a short follow-up film was shown, giving a word of testimony and extending an invitation to viewers to enter the counseling room for personal contact. During one season 30,000 people entered the pavilion and several thousand requested personal counseling. More than 4,000 copies of the French New Testament were given to these inquirers and a supply of English material was also distributed.

CANADIAN CENTENNIAL

The Fellowship of Evangelical Baptist Churches in Canada was interested in making a special appeal during Canada's centennial year. The Canadian Home Bible League, together with a committee representing these churches, made up a special Scripture booklet entitled, *100 Questions for Canada's 100th Birthday.* This was very well received and more than 100,000 homes were reached through its distribution.

The Young Calvinist Federation, also interested in providing a special centennial appeal, prepared a Scripture booklet called, *Behold the Answer,* and 60,000 homes received these booklets.

A group of Christian Reformed Churches provided the funds for a centennial edition of the French New Testament. This was distributed among French-speaking people, mostly in the Province of Quebec. More than 10,000 copies were placed in French-speaking homes.

A great number of churches - Baptist, Christian and Missionary Alliance, and Pentecostal - had special editions of Testaments and Scripture portions prepared for distribution during the centennial year. The Pentecostal Assembly of Canada launched one of its largest campaigns in Quebec. The World Home Bible League prepared a special edition of the Gospel of John for that program.

The work among the French-speaking people was most encouraging and it was soon discovered that the entrance of God's Word gives light. Many of those who received the French Gospels and Testaments were priests, nuns, and altar boys who gladly accepted them. Many conversions were reported.

ISLAND CAMPAIGNS

A group of pastors and laymen, most of them from Southern Baptist churches, participated in a preaching crusade in Jamaica from January 22 to February 4, 1968. The World Home Bible League furnished 5,000 Gospels of John, 5,000 New Testaments, and 3,000 copies of *God Speaks.* All the material had specially designed covers. The crusade was directed by the Reverend Todd Taylor who reported great success. Mr. Tony Klingenberg, our Southern Baptist representative, also accompanied the men.

SCRIPTURES FOR SERVICEMEN

Early in 1967 officers of the Christian Reformed Laymen's League approached the World Home Bible League and asked us to participate in a Vietnam "Thank-you" project. The organization, with its president, Dr. Robert Plekker of Hudsonville, Michigan, was prepared to provide for U.S. combat troops in Vietnam 100,000 packets containing various items such as socks, towelettes, pre-sweetened Kool-Aid, pencils, and a copy of the Gospel. The League was asked to cooperate in providing the Gospel of Mark. A Gospel was printed the cover of which depicted a soldier in front of a cross. To date more than 450,000 of the packets have been distributed overseas in Vietnam. In addition, fifty thousand complete servicemen's Testaments in the paraphrased edition were distributed to Vietnam combat troops through chaplains. These were also provided by the World Home Bible League, in cooperation with Tyndale House, publishers of *The Living Testament.*

In January, 1968, one of our board members, Mr. Martin Ozinga, accompanied the director, Mr. William Ackerman, to Vietnam to test the reaction of the boys in the field to these packets and to do some preliminary work in investigating possible distribution avenues. The project received the endorsement of many men, including Pat Boone, the singer, who said, "The Scriptures have meant a great deal through the ages to those in special danger - the words of comfort and of counsel - the story of Jesus Christ is helping to sustain thousands yet today and who has greater need for the Bible's message of hope than the men on the front lines in Vietnam. The Gospel of Mark is an exciting and precious part of the packet and gives it everlasting value."

Other endorsements were received from such dignitaries

as the President of the United States, Richard M. Nixon, Lyndon B. Johnson, Hubert Humphrey, George Romney, and others.

The packets also included a little card on which the recipients could order additional supplies. Among the items listed was a copy of the New Testament. Thousands of letters were received telling of the effectiveness of the project and expressing appreciation for the little Gospel, and at least 5,000 *Good News for Modern Man* Testaments were sent to combat troops in Vietnam through the World Home Bible League's sponsorship.

REACHING THE RUSSIANS

The most recent effort by the World Home Bible League to reach Russian people with the Scriptures was made possible through the Grand Rapids - South Women's Division, of which Mrs. Arnold Brink is president. In a very enthusiastic campaign these woman raised a sufficient amount of money to provide $5000.00 worth of Bibles to be distributed through Brother Andrew of "God's Smuggler" fame. These Scriptures will be distributed by underground associates to communistic countries. These women also were instrumental in raising additional funds which made possible the publication of the Book of Mark and the Book of Romans in a paraphrased edition. These two books were translated into Russian by Tyndale House, publishers of Living Letters.

Some years before this the League underwrote the reading of the Scriptures to Russian people. This effective ministry was carried out for more than one year in cooperation with the Temple Time broadcast of the Reformed Church of America.

INCIDENTS IN OUR SPANISH MINISTRY

THE LITTLE BLACK BOOK

Many years ago the League began distributing Spanish New Testaments. Before we printed our own, a black-covered Testament was purchased. These were distributed during the first season among Mexican migratory workers and workers from Puerto Rico. The workers were very happy to receive these Testaments and our supply could hardly keep up with the demand.

When the second migratory season arrived a problem was encountered. Migratory workers refused to receive the Testaments as readily as the group had the previous year. After a while we discovered that the priest had been so alarmed at the great number of Testaments that had come back into the country with the past season's migrants that all the new migrants had been warned, "Watch out for the man with the little black book."

So we began to print the New Testament with a bright red jacket. These Testaments were enthusiastically received and the problem disappeared.

More than fifteen years ago the World Home Bible League began to feel the necessity of owning its own printing plates. There was a particular need for Spanish plates in order to print the entire New Testament, which meant that more than $10,000 had to be raised for the printing plates and the first edition.

Prior to this time we had been purchasing these

Testaments from an existing Bible distribution agency. The cost to the League for each Testament was forty-five cents and when special inserts were included, the cost increased. Many of these Testaments were shipped to the migratory workers in the United States.

The work among the migrants was so richly blessed by God that it became the key to opening up new areas for foreign distribution. Some of the migrants had come from Mexico, others from Puerto Rico, and now a problem arose to supply both the domestic and foreign challenges.

It was becoming more and more evident that in order to distribute more books the unit price of each Testament had to be reduced. It was discovered that once we owned our own printing plates, which would cost $6,270, the unit price of the Testament would come to less than forty cents a copy. Further editions of the Testament could be had at an even more reasonable figure. The Holland-Zeeland chapter of the World Home Bible League, of which Mr. Tony Klingenberg was chairman at that time, accepted the challenge to raise the money. This was done by the churches in the Holland-Zeeland area contributing on a free-will offering basis. Soon the $6,270 was raised. The League now was able to have made the first printing plates in its history.

When the type was all set and the plates made, mats were pressed from the type and the original plates were put in a safe place. These plates were never actually used in the process of printing, but several matrices were made. The first printing was received a few months later and it represented a milestone in our ministry.

The World Home Bible League owes much to the missionaries employed in the Holland-Zeeland area of Michigan. It was their vision to reach the migratory workers that helped spark the distribution of the Word of

God to Spanish-speaking people. Many of the areas in North America were canvassed under the direction of such men as the Reverend Chester Schemper, Dr. David Vila, and Mr. Everett Vander Brink. A ministry was begun that was to have an effect on much of Mexico, Puerto Rico, and the Spanish-speaking world.

We had made progress. The cost of the Testament had been reduced to a price that we could more readily afford to pay, but we were still looking for ways and means of further reducing this cost. When involved in spending other people's money, expecially those who have given funds from very small incomes, you are constantly reminded of your responsibility to God. In the course of investigating possible ways of cutting the cost of Spanish Testament production, it was discovered that Testaments could be printed very reasonably in Mexico City. In order to do this, however, special plates had to be sent down there.

The League faced a problem here. Shipping the plates to Mexico City meant a long hazardous journey overland. Freight to Mexico had been known to be pilfered many times. To ship the plates by air would necessitate placing a heavy insurance value on them in case of loss.

After some deliberation it was decided to send the plates by air freight. One of the airlines serving Mexico City was contacted and with a little searching it was ascertained that this airline had never lost a plane between Chicago and Mexico City. Certainly, it was reasoned, God wouldn't let the one plane go down with our printing plates. We sent them that way and soon the presses in Mexico City were turning out the Spanish Testament.

We discovered, though, that this wasn't the best move either, but by this time the distribution had multiplied to such an extent that the antiquated equipment then available in Mexico City could not keep up with the demand placed upon us by missionaries. However, we did achieve a breakthrough in producing a pocket-sized Spanish New Testament for approximately twenty cents apiece. When we attempted to raise the money for these plates, one of our critics said, "What do you have to have printing plates for? Many of the Bible societies have Spanish Testament plates. You don't have to have another set." In a very short time, the answer became obvious - the Testaments were now costing us twenty cents. Every copy turned out saved us twenty-five cents over our original cost. We were reaching homes in Mexico and around the Spanish-speaking world for twenty cents a copy, or four cents an individual.

Today the World Home Bible League owns many sets of printing plates. There are at least two sets of Spanish New Testament and Bible plates here in the U.S.A. A complete set of New Testament plates owned by the World Home Bible League is in Spain. An additional set is in Mexico. One set of printing plates was in Cuba but is presumed lost or confiscated.

At the time of this writing the World Home Bible League has published more than one million Testaments from these plates.

A VISIT TO CUBA

Shortly after Fidel Castro came into power in Cuba, two members of the World Home Bible League, the Rev. Chester Schemper and our director, William Ackerman, visited the island. Ministerial meetings were held from the eastern tip of Cuba to the western province.

Visits were also made to jails where a great number of red-covered Testaments, produced by the World Home Bible League, were distributed. An amazing number of testimonies were given to these men by pastors and missionaries. It seemed as though the Holy Spirit had moved in a very effective way. Countless thousands of politicians and others had been thrown into prison. Everything they possessed had been taken away from them; they faced a bleak future and probable death. They clung to the teachings of the Scripture distributed to them, and many were the stories of conversion and renewed hope and faith in God.

One of the most remarkable stories concerned an eighteen-year old lad who spoke with our representatives at the large Santa Clara prison. He gave the following testimony:

"I have been sentenced to fifteen years at hard labor for the part I played in tormenting a supporter of the Castro regime. I am very sorry for this, but I want you to know that I am not sorry I got caught." When he was asked why he was not sorry that he was caught, his reply was startling. "Why, if I had not been caught I never would have met the missionary. If I had never met the missionary he would never have given me this little red Testament. If I had never read this little red Testament, I would never have met Jesus."

During this tour of Cuba our director was asked to speak at a ministerial gathering in Havana. A representative from another Bible distribution group was present. This group was committed to the selling of Scripture and was very much opposed to the free distribution carried out by the World Home Bible League. Directly after the presentation, this representative stood up and denounced free Bible distribution. He said it was wasteful and ridiculous. The violent manner in which he spoke against the League's program seemed to indicate his belief that the only Scripture the Holy Spirit would ever bless would be a Scripture that was sold.

No sooner had this man sat down when an Anglican

pastor arose. Our director was sure there would be another on slaught, but the man spoke very zealously and told the following story:

"A man walked out of a tavern under the influence of drink. In fact, he was so drunk he stumbled out of the tavern right into the hands of a colporteur who was selling Bibles. The colporteur offered to sell him a Bible and in his drunken stupor the man did not resist the sale. Barely able to make his way over to the curb he sat down and began to read, but it was not for him, and he threw the Bible down in the gutter in disgust.

"Along came another man," the Anglican continued. He picked up the Bible and read it and was soundly converted." In fact, he was a leading member in this Anglican pastor's church. "So you see," concluded the pastor, "sometimes God uses even a Bible that is thrown away in a gutter."

CUBA – A UNIQUE DISTRIBUTION

Cuba was one of the most fertile areas in the world for the sowing of the gospel. We met men and women there who were burdened over the souls of men, and reports reach us even today that some of the red-covered Testatments distributed years ago are still being used in that nation.

We shall never forget a pastor we met in a town in western Cuba. God gave him a tremendously interesting idea in Scripture distribution. It is the only time we ever met a man who tried this plan although, as we think it over, it certainly has many benefits.

This missionary wrote to us and obtained 200 Spanish New Testaments. He did not give them away, he did not sell them; instead he went from door to door in a town and offered to loan a copy to anyone who would read it. Then he returned to pick up the Testament two weeks later. This was extremely clever. First of all, there was an original contact made. Second, the man already provided the perfect excuse to call back. When he called back he would ask if they had read it. He would ask them questions about it. He would witness to them and invite them to his church. He would help them in understanding the Scripture and, if a genuine interest were displayed, he would offer to give them the Testament free of charge. It was a tremendously effective way of distribution.

MEXICO — TOO PRECIOUS A BOOK

A missionary in Sonora, Mexico, had given a League Scripture to a woman who was married to a fanatic believer in another religion. This woman realized that her husband had a very violent temper. She was very fearful of what would happen if he ever discovered the Testament, so she hid it behind a large picture that hung in her kitchen. One night it was accidentally jarred and the Testament fell down. The husband picked up the Book and a violent quarrel ensued. He then beat his wife and burned the Testament.

The missionary who had placed this Testament met the woman some time later. She told him the story. Expressing sympathy with the woman over the problem, and knowing her desire to have a Testament, he offered her another one. Very eagerly she accepted it and put it in another hiding place. This was also discovered. Another beating ensued and the second Testament was burned.

After many months the missionary met the woman and once again offered her another copy. She thanked him and smiled and said, "I would very much like to have one, but it is too precious a Book to be burned, so I will wait until I convert my husband."

MEXICO ALONG THE TAMESI RIVER

For many years the World Home Bible League has

82

supplied Bibles, Testaments, and Scripture portions to missionaries who work with the Tampico Boat Mission. Along the river, stretching from Tampico inland, there are a great number of people whose only contact with the rest of the world is the winding river. Passenger boats bring people up and down. Other boats bring groceries and supplies. Each day, weather permitting, the boat owned by the Tampico Mission traverses these waters to bring the Gospel to men and women living in humble huts. Many of them have never been more than five miles away from where they were born. Mr. Abe Marcus, the missionary, often went to preach, sometimes to distribute medical supplies, but above all to give them the Word of God. He told of stopping at a home at which he left a witness and then gave a New Testament upon the promise that it would be read. The man did not intend to keep his promise, but he put the Book on a shelf and forgot about it. One night his married son came home drunk and beat his wife and children. The father went to the shelf, got down the Book, reprimanded his son and told him to read the Testament. The son slipped off into the night.

Several months later a man signaled to the missionary boat. Mr. Marcus headed to the shore. It was the son who had been a drunkard. He told his story and said that the Testament had changed his life. He was no longer a drinker and did not beat up his wife and children, and now he wanted to know if he could be baptized.

One Sunday morning some weeks later a minister baptized this young man along the river. Another one of God's trophies was brought to Jesus' feet through the reading of a New Testament.

MEXICO – A BRIDE AND GROOM

A young couple who lived in one of the small villages of Mexico was about to be married. The father of the groom offered them a little hut that had been discarded many months before. It was a very humble place with no windows and no door, but at least it was a place to begin. The happy pair went up the mountainside to clean out the house. While cleaning a little shelf, a dust-covered booklet was dislodged and fell to the ground. It was picked up and on the cover was the title, *Dios Habla.* Through the reading of this little Spanish booklet, *God Speaks,* the couple was converted - converted through the Word of God in the form of a booklet which cost two cents. It had been read by someone else and discarded, but it still possessed the power to tell young people of Jesus.

In a village nearby a man loaned his friend a copy of this little book. A letter was later received stating, "I was saved while reading the little booklet called *Dios Habla,* which was loaned to me by a friend."

How true it is that the Word of God is still quick and powerful and sharper than any two-edged sword.

JESUS OF THE BOOK

About twenty years ago a Mexican man and his wife, together with their family of six children, came to Holland, Michigan. They had come from Texas to work in the pickle fields. A copy of the World Home Bible League Spanish New Testament was given to the mother, and the missionary who gave the Testament soon became a friend to the family. They began to attend the church services held for migratory workers in Borculo. As the maple trees began to take on their beautiful fall colors these Mexican workers headed back to their native state and the missionary was not sure whether he would ever see them on earth again.

The next summer as the missionary was working on the farms contacting migratory workers, a young boy came running to him. The missionary immediately recognized him as one of the six children of this Mexican family. The young boy, after enthusiastically greeting the missionary, could not wait to take the missionary to a field in which his mother was working.

The missionary exchanged greetings but the moment the Mexican woman's eyes fell upon the missionary she burst into tears. She took the turkish towel that covered her head, buried her face in it and sobbed. The missionary waited patiently. Soon she regained control of her emotions and then she blurted out the story of what had happened.

Soon after they had worked in the pickle fields of the Holland area, they found employment in the eastern area of Michigan where they worked for several weeks harvesting sugar beets. It was there that one of their children contracted a fatal disease. Still mourning the loss of the child, they returned to their home in Texas. Almost without warning, the husband of the family became very sick and died. The widow was then very dependent upon an eighteen-year-old daughter. She was faithful to her mother and a loving child. One day, this pride and joy of the household was carrying out some household chores. She was about to lift a can supposedly containing kerosene to the stove. There was a terrifying explosion. Later it was discovered that the daughter had mistaken a can of gasoline for a can of kerosene. The daughter lived only a short while.

The missionary found it difficult to control his own emotions, and his heart went out to the mother. He could understand the occasion for her uncontrollable grief. He realized that the experiences of the past months were indeed crushing. It was then that he asked the Lord to direct.

Before he could say anything the woman came out with

a statement of her own. It was a statement that made the missionary thank God. The exact words of it have long been lost in the pickle patch of the open fields of Michigan, but as close as the missionary could recall, the testimony of the lady was this: "Even though I have lost my husband and two children, I want you to know that the Jesus of the Book you gave me is the Friend who is always near. He means so very much to me."

This missionary stated, "I was thrilled at this woman's testimony. I was thrilled too because I was a sower of the Word and I was happy to know that the Spirit had blessed this ministry in the life of this migrant worker which was fraught with so many difficulties. I could tell by the way she told me of Jesus that it did not come merely from her lips but that it originated deep within her heart."

There is a sequel to the story that reveals without a doubt her true attitude and conviction concerning the value of Bible distribution.

In a building in that immediate area a service was held for the migrant workers. This woman and the remaining members of her family were all present for the service. An offering was taken. It was explained that this offering would help pay for Bibles and Testaments given to migrant workers through the ministry of the World Home Bible League.

A deacon who took the offering noticed that when the plate was passed this widow dropped in a ten-dollar bill. Ten dollars was a lot of money, representing a great deal of hard work in the open fields. Many times Mexicans, not familiar with American currency, made errors. The deacon called the matter to the attention of the woman and reminded her that this was a ten-dollar bill. She smiled and assured him that she had not made a mistake. She told him she wanted that money to go to the organization that provided the Testament for her. She wanted other people too to know Jesus who was her friend.

A VERY STRANGE STORY FROM CUBA

Most of the reports that came from pastors and Christian laymen were well substantiated, even though at times some of them seemed to border on the unbelievable. However, the following story was checked by the director many years ago when he visited Cuba. A Pilgrim Holiness pastor accompanied Mr. Ackerman on a visit to an old man who had previously received a red New Testament. He related in Spanish an interesting story translated as follows:

One day as he sat in the little courtyard in back of the rest home where he lived he began to think of his favorite niece who lived in Spain. He had corresponded with her and had some photos of her. He thought very highly of this young lady. He became strangely obsessed by the idea that she too should have one of the red Testaments, for probably she had never read any portion of the Bible. Several obstacles, however, confronted him. First, he did not have another Testament. Secondly, if he had the Testament how would he ever get it to her? He was penniless and had no way of even mailing it. The old man prayed about the matter constantly. The next time the minister came to call he explained the burden on his heart and asked the pastor if he could please have another Testament. The Testament was provided. After the pastor left the old man prayed to God again and explained that he didn't have any money and that he had not wanted to ask the pastor for any, but would He somehow enable him to get this Testament to his niece?

The next day there was bright sunshine and a pleasant breeze from the blue Caribbean Sea. The old man decided to look at the various ships docked in the harbor. A twenty-minute walk brought him there. He looked at the flags on the ships' masts. Some had come from far places on the other side of the world, others had come from countries in Europe. Finally he spotted a ship that had a Spanish flag flying on its mast. As he stood there with a prayer on his heart a young sailor came walking toward him and greeted him in Spanish. The old man returned the greeting and they began an interesting conversation. It developed, much to the old man's surprise, that the sailor lived only a few blocks away from his niece. In fact, he said he knew her. When he was asked whether or not he would be willing to give the package to the young lady the seaman assured the old man that he was willing to do so. And he did.

In a marvelous way God had provided that this Spanish Testament, a gift from an old man in Cuba, would get into the hands of the niece on the other side of the ocean.

Unfortunately it was impossible to follow up the story any further. Castro came and Cuba closed. The last thing we heard was that a thank-you note had been received by the old man. We do not know what happened after that, but we are confident that the God who can work out a problem like this in such a mysterious way can certainly incline the heart of this niece to accept the truth of the Holy Scripture.

This story was later filmed. The pastor who placed the Testament and the old man were both depicted and this testimony of God's provision was told through this film to tens of thousands of people across the U.S.A. and Canada.

Many times in our church services we sing the old familiar song, "God moves in a mysterious way His wonders to perform." One of the lessons we learned in the ministry of the World Home Bible League was that this is an absolute truth. We are continually reminded of His

88

faithfulness moving throughout the ministry in ways that constantly surprise us and even at times appear to be mysterious.

WILLING HANDS HELP WITH THE TASK

Very early in the history of the League interested persons began to give of their time and effort toward its success. Although it is impossible to recall all of those who had a contribution to make in time and interest, we remember Mr. and Mrs. Chester Evers and family, Mr. and Mrs. Louis Vree, and Mr. and Mrs. Sam Postmus. I can also recall that my wife and son, and some of our neighbors and friends, too, gathered nightly in our basement to help unpack and pack Bible cartons. When the ministry first started I purchased Bibles with no special markings and inserted a page giving instructions on Bible reading as well as the address of the then American Home Bible League.

The World Home Bible League is very grateful that God has continued to incline the hearts of many people to provide volunteer services.

Many years ago, one of our board members volunteered to transport all the Bibles printed in Cleveland, Ohio, to our headquarters in Chicago. When the trucks arrived late on Saturday evening we called in volunteers from the local churches, who eagerly responded and unloaded them. It was necessary to have special racks built in our old storage area. A carpenter volunteered his services and provided the labor free of charge. In all the years that we occupied our building in Roseland, Chicago, almost all the fuel oil was donated by a Christian businessman, and when he passed on his wife continued this practice. The heating plant in our previous building and our entire air-conditioning plant were also donated by local businessmen.

Through our women's division more than 25,000 used Bibles have been repaired and rebound. Twenty-two thousand of these Bibles have been sent to Africa. This meant a saving to the League of at least $25,000 because each repaired Bible is worth at least one dollar to the League.

Many have volunteered to collect world banks in their areas. One woman in Wisconsin has been doing this for the past twelve years and has been instrumental in bringing thousands of dollars into the World Home Bible League's ministry.

Many women in the Chicago area and in Michigan are actively engaged, on a volunteer basis, in correcting our Bible correspondence courses. Thousands of courses have been corrected and the lessons cheerfully picked up and delivered to our South Holland address.

Many individuals catching the spirit of the volunteer work and wishing to cooperate in one way or another have loaned us money, without interest, so that our new headquarters could become a reality. Many merchants have donated, or given us at cost, supplies and services to make our new home in South Holland possible.

The missionaries who distribute the Word at home and abroad are also to be considered volunteers. They receive no pay for the actual distribution of the Testaments. Our board members also give of their time freely. Many have traveled on League business at no expense to the League.

When we consider all this volunteer help, plus the economy of operating our own bindery, we can truthfully state that the Christian's dollar is being stretched further than ever before. Taking into consideration the use of volunteer help, we can conservatively state that tens of thousands of free hours of consecrated work have been donated as unto Christ.

OPERATION HANDCLASP

Today, under the capable leadership of Mr. Ralph Vander Zee, we are making use of volunteers as never before. When the World Home Bible League's first canvass took place on the streets of Walkerton in 1938, forty-five Bibles were distributed and at the time we felt that this was a large number. As the ministry continued to grow, and many missionaries and pastors became interested in our program, requests for a thousand or five thousand Testaments at once became quite common-place. Then we were startled to hear of figures as high as one hundred thousand, one-half million and even one million, which I felt was out of the question. How could we ever provide Bibles in such tremendously large quantities? Again our faith was small and again God had to teach us that in His good time the way would be prepared for us to meet even such staggering challenges.

In the providence of God a Christian printer in South Holland, Illinois, became interested in reproducing the Scripture on a press he had recently acquired. It was an offset printing press capable of producing as many as 10,000 to 12,000 complete booklets per hour, and it was inevitable that this Christian printer and the World Home Bible League should begin working together. One of the first productions was the publication of a Scripture booklet in the Tiv language of Nigeria. More than 250,000 of these were printed. Shortly after this we were able to produce 200,000 English Gospels of John for the "New Life for All Program" launched by the evangelical missionaries of Nigeria (SIM and SUM).

As we began to produce these in this quantity, problems arose in the binderies. We were constantly flooding them with such large orders that they had difficulty handling the work and although we began to produce the Bibles very economically, the cost of binding was high. One day, while our director was having lunch with several ministers in South Holland, Illinois, they began discussing the printing and production of Bibles, and God gave them the idea to begin a volunteer program, later to be called "Operation Handclasp." The idea was that various churches in the nearby community would be solicited. They would be asked to provide volunteer workers. These workers would come to a building in which equipment would be set up and at this building the Bibles could be put together, bound, and trimmed.

We approved the plan and began with the use of a small onion barn. This barn did not have running water and, therefore, no sanitary facilities. Would the volunteers come out under such circumstances? There were crude wooden tables, a few electric staple machines and a huge quantity of work. It was, as somebody put it later, "a Robert Hall experience in religion," - no fancy fixtures, no fancy tables. A few churches responded. Then the news leaked out and more and more churches responded and eventually "Operation Handclasp" became one of the major facets of our ministry.

The spirit of those who came out was most encouraging. They felt that this was their work and they were delighted to handle the Bibles that would be placed in the huts of Nigeria and in the jungles of South America. They knew they were having an important and vital part in communicating the gospel through the Printed Page.

Today, more than forty churches, representing many denominations, send volunteer workers to participate in our binding operation. The Lord has blessed the work so that we have had to move twice, and are now in our third location which is a large building in back of our general administrative building along the Calumet Expressway in South Holland.

One day one of our staff members got out of his car. It had been raining and as a large car came by at a fast rate of speed, water splashed all over as the woman driver suddenly put on the brake, slammed the car door, and ran into the "Operation Handclasp" building. Our staff member recognized her as one of the faithful volunteers and he inquired, "Is something wrong?"

"Something wrong?" she exclaimed. "Yes, I am late for work at Handclasp."

One of the groups that came out in the evening was from a Negro Baptist church in Chicago. They represented a hard-working group of Christians. It was a real privilege to see them respond to the invitation to get the Word out. A rather heavy-set Negro woman was usually in charge. Standing there one night, I watched them at their work. As they were about to go home I thanked them for coming and this woman, who was also the spokesman for the group, said, "Don't thank us. It is a real privilege to work here," and then she said, "Let's pray." She bowed her head and began to pray and among the things she said that thrilled my heart was, "Dear Lord, we thank you for the privilege of being able to work here to produce all these Scriptures to go to the uttermost parts of the world."

Many who have faithfully worked here have also been faced with the burden of the financial need. Several substantial gifts have been given that have enabled us to pay for sorely needed equipment. A woman who worked at our "Operation Handclasp" donated money to pay for 25,000 copies of the Scripture. One retired man faithfully comes in every morning and works on a particular machine giving his time as unto the Lord, proud to be a member of

This is the first home canvassed by Mr. and Mrs. William A. Chapman on a Good Friday afternoon in the year 1938. It was one of 245 homes called on at Walkerton, Indiana.

CHICAGO — The Seamen's Mission is operated and sponsored by a number of churches in the Chicagoland area. It serves those whose ships dock at the Calumet Harbor. All of the Scripture supplied for distribution are given by the World Home Bible League.

MEXICO — After the first ecumenical meeting in Rome, the Roman Catholic church became very interested in Scripture distribution. Bishop Mendez of Cuernavaca, Mexico, contacted the League on several occasions. Conferences were held and distribution of Scriptures resulted. Bishop Mendez, Mr. Ackerman, and others posed for this picture in 1968.

In the fall of 1968 ground breaking ceremonies were held at the site of our new international headquarters in South Holland. Left to right, Rev. Warren Hietbrink, Mr. William Ackerman, International Director, Mr. Chester Evers, Sr., Mr. Herman Chapman, and Mr. William Chapman, Founder.

Mr. William A. Chapman, founder, and Mr. C. L. Evers who joined him early in the work, examine the first copies of the Spanish Testaments printed by the World Home Bible League.

An early Bible distribution committee meeting. Note the Bibles stacked in the form of a pyramid. This distribution was under the supervision of a local ministerial group and took place in Michigan very early in the ministry of the American Home Bible League.

Many of the church area canvasses took place in Michigan. This group of people from the Bethel Reformed Church of Holland, Michigan, are ready to go out and offer Scriptures under the supervision of their pastor, the Rev. John Van Harn. Rev. Van Harn later became the League's Church Relations Director and his wife became the National Women's Division President.

Mr. and Mrs. William Chapman and Dr. and Mrs. Eugene Heideman in Vellore, South India, in 1964. Dr. Heideman was director of the India Home Bible League in the early 1960's.

The author and his wife, and Mr. and Mrs. Chester L. Evers, Sr., visited Japan to meet the workers there. This meeting took place in Fukuoka in 1958. Seated, left to right, the Rev. Boude C. Moore, Mr. and Mrs. William A. Chapman, Mrs. Chester L. Evers. Standing, left to right, Mr. Shun Suzuki, former director of the Japan Home Bible League, and Mr. Chester L. Evers, Sr.

One of the most extensive Scripture distribution campaigns was in the greater San Diego, California area. The original contact with the San Diego County Council of Churches was made by Chester L. Evers, Sr. The Rev. Billy Graham gave the opening address and the following Sunday all the churches cooperated through the local ministerial association to bring the Word to the entire county of San Diego. Left to right, Mr. William Ackerman, Rev. Billy Graham, Dr. Wayne A. Neal, Executive Secretary San Diego Ministerial Association.

The author shows one of our first bank collectors some of the many letters that have come in requesting Bibles for distribution. Pictured, left to right, Mr. Anthony Klingenberg, Mr. Nicholas Tanis, and Mr. William A. Chapman.

Tours of World Home Bible League facilities are encouraged. A group of ladies from the Holland-Zeeland, Michigan area chartered buses and spent an enjoyable afternoon becom

A group of seminary students from Western Theological Seminary in Holland, Michigan, came to the League office for a work assignment of Scripture distribution in Chicago. Seminarians under the direction of Dr. John Piet were stationed at the airport, Rush Street, Pacific Garden Mission, and the railroad stations. It was a practical work assignment that was remembered for a long time.

Several of our Board members accompanied the Seminarians on their Chicago assignment.

...g acquainted with the operation of the World Home Bible League in South Holland, ...nois.

At the World Home Bible League's twenty-fifth anniversary meeting, held at the Winona Lake Conference Grounds, Mrs. Herman Chapman(daughter-in-law) former Women's Division president, pins a corsage on Mrs. William Chapman.

Mr. Douwe Tamminga, who prayed at the bedside of Mr. Chapman, became one of our first bank ambassadors after his retirement from International Harvester Company. "Old Douwe" was a familiar sight calling on homes in the Roseland (Chicago) area for many years. Upon his retirement he was given a token of appreciation. Here Mr. Chapman presents the gift to him. A memorial for Mr. Tamminga can be seen at our League headquarters.

At the fifteenth anniversary of the League Mr. and Mrs. Chapman were given a gold Bible. Special pages were flown to the various foreign fields and each director wrote words of greeting and signed them. These pages were then bound into this Bible. Representatives from east, west, north, and south came from the Moody Bible Institute to be at this presentation. Rev. Gary DeWitt (far right) officiated.

TORONTO, CANADA — In 1969 the Canadian Home Bible League opened a new office. Under the supervision of Mr. John Vander Boom, Director, the work has flourished across Canada and the League has been of tremendous help to thousands of churches. Left to right, Miss Ann Ysinga, Mrs. Nell Schaafsma, Rev. Fred Tiessen, Mrs. Jo Vander Boom, Mr. John Vander Boom, Mrs. Marian Injerd, Mr. William Ackerman, Mrs. Tena Enter.

Many church groups arrange for tours of the League's facilities. In this photo Mrs. Herman Chapman, daughter-in-law of the founder, explains a piece of printing equipment to a visiting group.

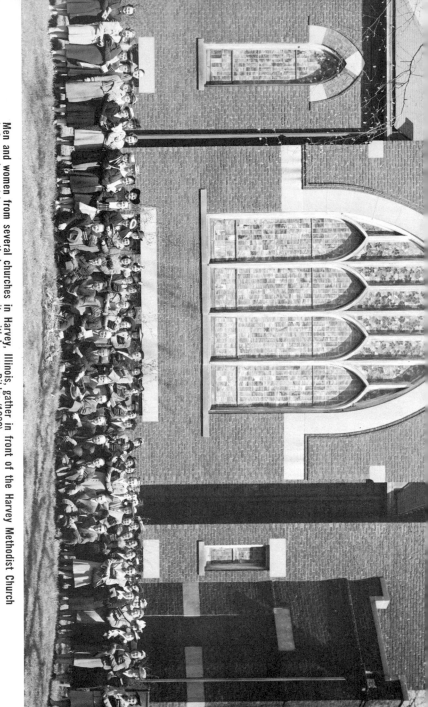

Men and women from several churches in Harvey, Illinois, gather in front of the Harvey Methodist Church before going out to canvass their community with League Bibles (1939).

Rev. Edward Wyman of the Nazarene Church in San Antonio, Texas, began reaching Spanish-speaking people through League Scriptures as early as 1945. He and many other missionaries have continued to distribute League Scriptures throughout these many years.

INDIA — Mr. Herman Chapman, son of Mr. William A. Chapman, stands beside a bullock cart which has transported tons of Scriptures for the India Home Bible League. Mr. Herman Chapman succeeded Chester L. Evers as president of the World Home Bible League in 1968.

Mrs. Celia V. Kastelyn, Right, was the first Director of the Women's Division in Chicago. She and Mrs. Siemke Otto presented many musical slide programs for the League throughout Chicagoland.

The first officers of the National Women's Division Board were L - R Mrs. John Van Harn, president; Mrs. John Huizenga, treasurer; Mrs. Albert Kruithoff, corresponding secretary; Mrs. Harry Zegarius, recording secretary; Mrs. Arthur Hoogstrate, vicar; Mrs. Herman Chapman, vice-president.

The enthusiastic representation to the Women's Division resulted in many bus loads of women attending the annual World Home Bible League Conference at Winona Lake.

THE WOMEN'S DIVISION

The Women's Division of the World Home Bible League was organized in the early 60's and began as a local Chicago area project. Soon it caught the imagination of women in Grand Rapids, Holland, and Zeeland, Michigan; and Pella and Northwest, Iowa. Later women in Wisconsin, New Jersey and Canada also began to organize local Divisions.

Among some of the women's special projects are:

The repairing of more than 25,000 used Bibles. These are eventually sent to Africa.

The correcting of Bible Correspondence courses sent to Ghana and other African countries. Many of the women also underwrote the cost of processing Bible correspondence students.

Later on the women became very interested in underwriting a number of dialects of the Scriptures. Various women's groups underwrote material for tribes in Mexico, South America, New Guinea, and other South Sea Islands.

Mrs. John Van Harn is the Director of the National Women's Division and was appointed to this position by our international Board.

Additional information on the women's work can be found throughout this book. Use the postcard inserted in this book to obtain further information on these activities.

One of the first committees of the Chicago Division. L - R Mrs. Genevieve Verbeek, Mrs. Esther Stell, Mrs. Sue Miedema, Mrs. Classina Tuinstra, Mrs. Celia Kastelyn, Mrs. Rique Evers.

Dear Reader:

This handy order card is enclosed for your convenience and we urge you to use it.

World Home Bible League
16801 Van Dam Road
South Holland, Illinois 60473

Please send me further information concerning:

- [ ] Materials available for Bible canvasses.
- [ ] Bible Studies material.
- [ ] Availability of speakers for church services, etc.
- [ ] World Bank program.
- [ ] Calendar program.
- [ ] The Sower.
- [ ] Wills and Annuities.
- [ ] Other _____

Please send me _____ additional copies of *Story Without An End.*

Name_____

Address _____
          Street Number
_____
City   State   Zip Code

Send it in today ▶

BUSINESS REPLY MAIL
No postage stamp necessary if mailed in the United States

POSTAGE WILL BE PAID BY

The World Home Bible League

16801 VAN DAM ROAD

SOUTH HOLLAND, ILLINOIS 60473

Dear Reader:

This handy order card is enclosed for your convenience and we urge you to use it.

World Home Bible League
16801 Van Dam Road
South Holland, Illinois 60473

Please send me further information concerning:

☐ Materials available for Bible canvasses.
☐ Bible Studies material.
☐ Availability of speakers for church services, etc.
☐ World Bank program.
☐ Calendar program.
☐ The Sower.
☐ Wills and Annuities.
☐ Other _____

Please send me _____ additional copies of *Story Without An End.*

Send it in today ▶

Name_____

Address _____
         Street Number

City   State   Zip Code

BUSINESS REPLY MAIL

No postage stamp necessary if mailed in the United States

POSTAGE WILL BE PAID BY

The World Home Bible League

16801 VAN DAM ROAD

SOUTH HOLLAND, ILLINOIS 60473

CANADA — In the northern area of Canada, a farmer's family receives a copy of the Scripture provided by the Canadian Home Bible League.

INDIA — The Evangelist Billy Graham pauses alongside a station wagon that advertises Bible correspondence courses in Vellore, India. The World Home Bible League supplied the textbook for these correspondence courses.

As the Scriptures are translated into tribal languages, we are grateful the conversions often result. These three young people from the Mixe tribe now attend the Bible Institute in Mexico which was directed by Rev. Roger Greenway.

Mr. Gerrit Smit, one of our workers at Operation Handclasp, processes an order for Spanish New Testaments to be distributed in South America.

Operation Handclasp has produced millions of Scriptures through the efforts of volunteer workers who have given thousands of hours of their time to produce Bibles, Testaments, and portions. The program is under the supervision of Mr. Ralph Vander Zee.

JAPAN—"Come unto me all ye that labor and are heavy laden and I will give you rest." The Rev. Maas Vander Bilt, director of the Japan Home Bible League, pauses alongside a road to give a heavily burdened woman a copy of GOD SPEAKS in the Japanese language.

JAPAN — (Billy Graham Evangelistic Crusade of 1967). The Rev. Edward Van Baak and Rev. Maas Vander Bilt at the Billy Graham Evangelistic rally in Tokyo, Japan, where the League distributed tens of thousands portions of the new Japanese Bible.

AUSTRALIA—Thousands of copies of the World Home Bible League Scripture were distributed through the Billy Graham evangelistic team in campaigns throughout the U.S.A. and the world. This placement of a large print New Testament took place in Australia.

IN A MOUNTAIN VILLAGE OF OLD MEXICO, Wycliffe Translator, Searle Hoogshagen, has worked for seventeen years in the production of the Scriptures in the Mixe dialect. The First Reformed Church of Roseland, of which Rev. Warren Hietbrink is pastor, is paying a substantial part of the publication cost.

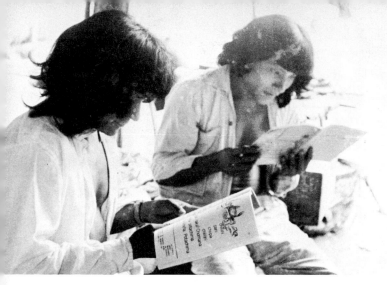

SOUTH SEA ISLANDS — Members of the Candoshi tribe of a South Sea Island read a Scripture pamphlet recently translated by the Wycliffe Bible Translators and published by Scriptures Unlimited, a joint venture of the World Home Bible League and New York Bible Society.

NEW GUINEA — An "informant" checks a manuscript in a tribal dialect of New Guinea. This is one of many translations underwritten by the League and the New York Bible Society under our Scriptures Unlimited program.

Dr. Cornelius Wierenga founded the India Home Bible League in 1950. The result was that millions of adults and children were given copies of the Scriptures in their own native language.

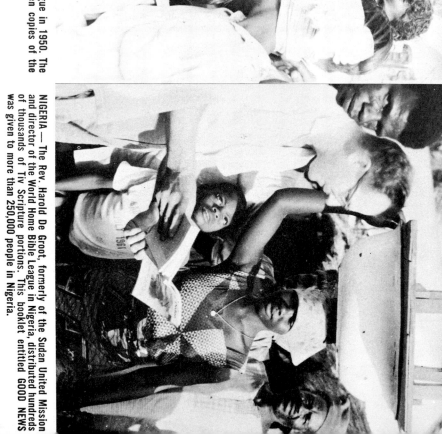

NIGERIA — The Rev. Harold De Groot, formerly of the Sudan United Mission and director of the World Home Bible League in Nigeria, distributed hundreds of thousands of Tiv Scripture portions. This booklet entitled GOOD NEWS was given to more than 250,000 people in Nigeria.

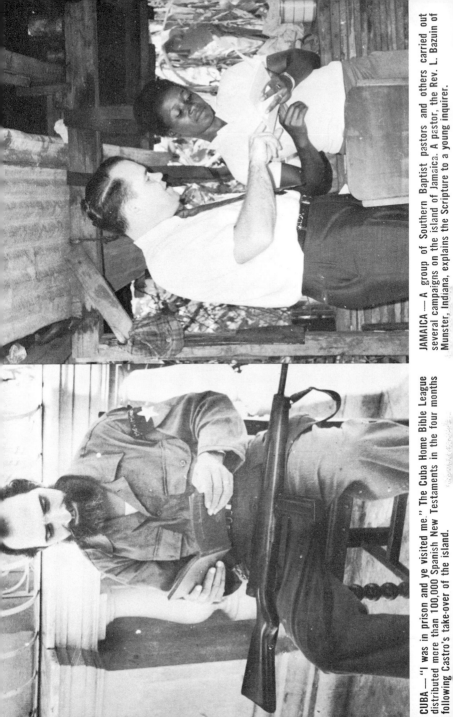

CUBA — "I was in prison and ye visited me." The Cuba Home Bible League distributed more than 100,000 Spanish New Testaments in the four months following Castro's take-over of the island.

JAMAICA — A group of Southern Baptist pastors and others carried out several campaigns on the island of Jamaica. A pastor, the Rev. L. Bazuin of Munster, Indiana, explains the Scripture to a young inquirer.

CEYLON—The Rev. John Van Ens, with his twin brother, Clarence, reached one million homes in Ceylon between the years of 1951 and 1968. Ceylon nationals now carry on the work they began.

OFF THE VANCOUVER ISLAND COAST — The good ship "Messenger III" owned by the Shantymen's Mission of Canada. Many cartons of Bibles were delivered by this ship to remote areas along Canada's rugged western coast.

A 20 year translation project involving the Sierra Juarez New Testament was finalized at a dedication ceremony in Oaxaca, Mexico. Wycliffe translators, Neal and Jane Nellis wrote that the presence of our W.H.B.L. founder and his wife at the dedication service meant much to them personally and was a time of encouragement to all. The funds for the publication of this Testament will be provided by Scriptures Unlimited.

The Scriptures Unlimited committee is comprised of four members of the New York Bible Society and four members of the World Home Bible League. Here they survey a very large amount of material shipped to Mexico for distribution throughout all of Latin America. Reading from left to right, Mr. Santos Galan (Manager of the Mexico office), Mr. Y. R. Kindberg, Director of the New York Bible Society, Mr. Herbert Johnson, board member, Mr. Herman Chapman, President, Mr. Jim Kubach, Vice-President, Mr. Ben Ottenhoff, Mr. Paul Baker, World Home Bible League board member, and Mr. William Ackerman.

One of the three objectives of Scriptures Unlimited is to produce a new Spanish translation of the Bible. Mr. John Beekman, Translation Coordinator, Wycliffe Bible Translators, (right) confers with Mr. Richard Anderson, Chief Translator of the Scriptures Unlimited Spanish project.

In Vellore, India, the India Home Bible League carried out extensive Bible correspondence course activity. At least 200,000 people took this Bible correspondence course written by Dr. John Piet.

LEBANON — This distribution of Arabic Scripture occurred in an old olive orchard where, many years ago, Jesus might have walked. Mr. Mitri Ziady, director of the League there, has been responsible for distribution to many Arabic speaking people.

MEXICO (Yucatan) — The Rev. Hans Weerstra places a large print Gospel of John in the Spanish language. Rev. Weerstra was instrumental in placing tens of thousands of Scriptures in the Yucatan peninsula campaign of 1970.

At Operation Handclasp, Testaments printed in the Spanish, English, Arabic, and other languages are bound.

VIETNAM — Mr. Martin Ozinga, board member, hands a Highland, Indiana, youth a thank-you packet. The 550,000 portions of Scripture that were included in these packets for Vietnam were provided by the World Home Bible League. This was a cooperative project of the Christian Reformed Laymen and the League.

OPERATION HANDCLASP

A group of enthusiastic young women volunteers are stapling Scripture booklets to be distributed in Texas by the Southern Baptist Ministerial Association.

the team that is helping to supply the Scripture at such reasonable cost. He has helped produce one and one-half million gospel portions!

It is impossible to list here all the material that has been produced at great savings, but in order to give you an idea, here are a few outstanding projects: Arabic New Testaments for distribution in such areas as Lebanon, Jordan, and the Arabian Gulf; Bulu New Testaments for the Cameroons in Africa; Sahu New Testaments to be distributed in Ethiopia.

More than three-quarters of a million booklets have been printed for the Airmail from God Mission. These booklets will be distributed by airplane in Central America, South America, and Mexico.

Hundreds of thousands of Testaments and tracts have been published in the Spanish language. Many of them were distributed at the 1968 Olympic games in Mexico City. Italian Gospels of John have been produced to be used among Italian-speaking people who reside in Canada. Large-print Gospels of John in English and Spanish have been produced. More than 150 churches have ordered personalized New Testaments printed with an invitation to attend church and a statement as to the hours of worship, etc.

As this work progressed more people became interested. A printer in Holland, Michigan, also produced material at very low cost. This material was shipped into South Holland for binding. One of the many interesting booklets published by this printer and bound by the World Home Bible League's "Operation Handclasp," was a paraphrased Gospel of John in the text of the *Living New Testament*. All in all, more than eight million copies of the Scripture have been produced as of January 1, 1969.

A man who visited "Operation Handclasp" turned to

our director and asked, "Do you have any specific need?" He was told that a large cutting machine for trimming books on three sides was sorely needed and that a used one could be obtained for $4,500.

"I will buy it for you," said the man.

A couple who contributed faithfully to the League over the years read about "Operation Handclasp" and donated two printing presses. A man and his wife toured the facilities and later gave more than $40,000. They told us the reason they gave was that when they saw all those people working, giving of their time so willingly, they felt this was one of the best places to make that type of an investment.

In many churches I have often referred to that familiar text of Habakkuk 2:14: "For the earth shall be filled with the knowledge of the glory of the Lord, as the waters cover the sea." Now, for the first time in my life I began to see how this was possible. Although it is hard to give an estimate, due to the various types of publications, paper, and cover material, we know that there is a tremendous savings in this operation. A Testament that costs us twenty cents would cost at least forty cents if produced elsewhere.

The number of Bibles we can produce here is almost unlimited. We invest thousands of dollars per week in "Operation Handclasp." Its output could be greatly increased but is limited only by the finances entrusted to us.

Another amazing thing is that the more Bibles we produce the more demands we get from missionaries to supply their needs. You would think that the time would eventually come when the demand for Scripture would diminish, but the supply never seems adequate to meet the demands.

CHARGE OR GIVE THEM AWAY

The World Home Bible League in its original objective had a vision of placing a Bible in every Bibleless home to win souls for Jesus Christ. It was taken for granted that the Scripture would be distributed free of charge. As the work expanded into foreign countries some missionaries felt that a small token should be given by those who received the Bibles. After studying this at some length the League determined that we were a service organization and, if the missionary in a given area felt that it was necessary to charge a small amount of money for the Scripture, we would approve such procedure. However, under no circumstances would we permit this to be done if price was a barrier to ownership. In other words, we were interested in getting the unchurched to read the Word of God. We were not particularly interested in receiving money from anyone for the Word and if he were too poor, under no circumstances should he be denied a Gospel, Testament, or a Bible.

This was in conflict with the firm policies of many existing Bible associations, which were strongly committed to the sale of Scripture and in some cases openly opposed our distribution projects. One example of the hostility generated came from a colporteur who stated that the Bible League's ministry was promoted by the forces of Satan because we were giving Scripture away and ruining his sales program. The heat of this argument abated somewhat but during the height of the difficulty the World Home Bible League, through its publication *The Sower,* set forth its policies in an editorial. The article introduced some very interesting aspects concerning Scripture distribution and its related problems. This editorial was entitled, "The Debate."

THE DEBATE

Ever since the first missionaries distributed Bibles, Testaments, or Gospel portions, the question arose, shall we charge for the Scriptures, or shall we give them away?

An association of Bible societies of which the World Home Bible League is *not a member* has gone on record as strongly favoring the sale of Scripture. Its report caustically questions the effectiveness of free distribution. In other parts of the world some who distribute the Scripture have taken such a strong stand on the subject of selling the Holy Scripture that it would appear at times that they doubt that the Holy Spirit can bless a portion of the Scripture given free of charge.

We like the philosophy set forth by the prophet Isaiah when he seems to shout in chapter 55:1, "Ho, every one that thirsteth, come ye to the waters, and he that hath no money; come ye, buy, and eat; yea, come, buy wine and milk without money and without price."

The World Home Bible League, after many years of Bible distribution experience and careful study, has come to definite conclusions concerning the sale and free distribution of the Scripture. Any organization that has honestly evaluated this problem cannot make an unreserved statement that all Scripture should be sold. Nor can any organization state that all Scripture distributed by them should be given away. Contributing factors that determine the proper distribution method are present in every situation. Among these are the economy of the nation in which the distribution takes place, the policy of the foreign missionary or mission organization in that nation, and the culture of those to whom the Bible will be distributed. In a person-to-person Scripture-placement ministry, almost every incident calls for individualized action.

Do you think that there is anything particularly commendable about selling a Bible? If so, Woolworth and the local department stores are doing a tremendous job. People buy Bibles for many reasons. Some buy them merely as gifts. Others buy them as showpieces. There have been men and women, I am sure, who have purchased Bibles for good-luck charms. Just selling Bibles for the purpose of making a sale or profit can hardly be construed as a missionary venture.

Frankly, the World Home Bible League is not interested in just selling another Bible. We are not interested in two Bibles in every home, but a Bible in every home of the world so that souls will be won for Christ.

The stand we have taken is a very costly one. If we could sell the Scripture we distribute instead of giving it away we would be in a most enviable position. Our budget would be almost twice what it is today; however, our conscience would bother us. If the Christian public donates funds for the distribution of God's Word, it expects that those Bibles, Testaments, and portions will be distributed free or at such an attractive token price that they will not be refused. Is it right to have anyone pay for a Bible twice? If a person sends a contribution so that a Bible can be given free and then the recipient is charged for that Bible, two people are paying for the Bible produced - the contributor and the recipient. The World Home Bible League refuses to be a part of this type of distribution.

One of the factors in determining policy in regard to distribution depends on the financial ability or inability of those who are about to receive the Scripture. It is still true that millions throughout the world do not earn sufficient money for the bare necessities of life. Bibles and Testaments in many nations are beyond the purchasing power of the poor and the desolate. Should these people be penalized because they are poor? Have we not been admonished, "Freely ye have received, freely give?" We at the World Home Bible League are determined that the poor of the world will not go without the Word of God because they cannot provide the money.

In recent years a story was told to us by a missionary who worked on a translation and after many years produced a New Testament in the language of the people. It was subsequently published and placed on sale through a bookstore. Shortly after publication, the missionary left the country and was away for twenty years. I was told that his work was not too well received for few had purchased it. The question came up, what shall we do with all these New Testaments that are left? These people were so brainwashed on the subject of selling New Testaments it never occurred to them that they could be given away. How many people died without Christ during the twenty years that this version of Scripture remained on the shelf? By what stretch of the imagination can anybody defend such a policy?

Some claim that it is much easier to give a Bible away than to sell it. This is not necessarily true. Under a strict sales policy the only requirement in the sale of Scripture is that the person to whom it is sold have the price. Once this mercenary action is taken the Bible is his absolute property. Regardless of how many Bibles he may have at home he can still purchase an additional one or two. The person is not indebted to anyone financially or morally to read them. This tends to commercialize distribution so that it almost becomes a mere business transaction. Many times under this system the ministry of the church is misunderstood when, after being introduced to the Word of God, someone is told that he has to pay for its message.

When a Bible is given free under the policies of the World Home Bible League there are at least three requirements to be met. First, there is no other Bible in the home. Second, there is a promise made to read the Bible placed. Third, wherever possible such placement must be made by a representative of the church.

Another favorite argument of those who insist on selling is that the Scripture represents a valued possession only when a price is attached. Something that is given away, they reason, is not worth anything in the opinion of the person who receives it. Is this logical? The deepest gratitude a human soul can experience is when someone who cannot possibly benefit himself by the transaction gives a token of love. Is it not true that some of your most treasured possessions are those for which you paid absolutely nothing? The diamond ring upon the finger of a married woman means much more to her because it was given to her. Could she possibly consider it to be of more value if she bought it herself? In the spiritual realm this is even more sharply defined. The gift of salvation, which is treasured by every Christian above all earthly possessions, is free, something not earned or paid for but a free gift of our gracious Father in heaven. Therefore, should not the motivating force in evangelism and Bible distribution be love, a love born of concern for men and women who are dying without Christ?

It can even be concluded that possibly there is more waste through the selling of the Scripture than through free distribution. It all depends on what you have for an objective. If you are interested in using the Bible as a tool of evangelism, you are interested in reaching the lost. If you are interested in merely increasing your Bible sales year by year, you don't care who receives the Scripture or for what purpose. Therefore, we are of the conviction that it is the Christian's responsibility to provide a copy of the Bible for every Bibleless home. We fail to see that it is the church's responsibility or the individual Christian's responsibility to be assured that every home has two Bibles or that every home has two different versions of the Bible.

In every battle there will be a loss of ammunition. It is also true that every inoculation by a missionary doctor does not take. Every sermon preached by a pastor does not result in the salvation of sinners. Every Testament sold or given away is not thoroughly read. By selling Bibles and Scripture portions you sow sparingly, but the Bible admonishes that those who sow sparingly shall also reap sparingly. Don't be concerned by a certain amount of seed that falls by the wayside. The parable of the sower predicted that. Thank God for the seed that bears fruit one hundredfold!

Our confidence is not in the sale or in the free distribution of the Scriptures, but it is in the God who told us that His Word shall never return unto Him void. We do not always favor free distribution nor do we always favor the sale of the Scripture. Our program is tailor-made for each area. Therefore, we do not bind ourselves to an ironclad rule for that would definitely restrict the effectiveness of our ministry.

THE WORLD BANK PROGRAM IS BORN

One of our board members who resided on the west side of Chicago arranged a meeting with his neighbor, Dr. Cornelius R. Wierenga, a missionary from India, who was home on what was to be his last furlough. On my way to this meeting I said to the person who accompanied me, "We'd better be careful today, because we don't want to get involved in such a great country as India." However, after listening to Dr. Wierenga we felt the concern that he radiated, and we could not help agreeing to do whatever we could.

He said, "If you can supply the Scripture to me so that I can distribute it in the villages in the Tamil and Telegu languages of southern India, I shall be able to reach more people in the next seven years of my ministry than in all my lifetime to date."

Our reply was, "Dr. Wierenga, with the help of God we will raise money for India." India was not an especially attractive country from the standpoint of solicitation of funds. At the time the evangelical world was focusing its attention on Japan. Without even the proverbial nickel in our treasury we pledged to Dr. Wierenga full support of his Scripture distribution program in India. At that time it was estimated it would not be more than $50 per month.

Shortly before Dr. Wierenga departed for India, he was invited to attend our annual meeting. He was given the first check for $700 with which to begin the work in a

103

small way. It was a momentous occasion for the League. It was a giant step into a strange foreign land, and God approved and sent His blessing. In a very short time the monthly $50 grew to $100, then to $500, and eventually to $1,000 per month. In addition to the contributions sent to Dr. Wierenga from the States, some money was raised through token contributions from some of the Scripture placements in India. The World Home Bible League soon acquired a very strong foreign affiliate destined to reach more than three million people throughout India.

With the needs before us of a country representing at that time about four hundred million people, new means had to be devised whereby we could raise sufficient sums of money to meet these challenges. I was confident that the God who had opened this avenue of great challenge would also take care of the need and He was about to do that very thing.

An urgent letter from Dr. Wierenga acknowledging God's blessing indicated the need for increased revenue. It came one day before our new international director, Mr. William Ackerman, arrived from the East. The following day we met with our wives at my summer home on Lake Dalecarlia in Indiana. After much discussion and prayer, the Lord revealed a new idea. We had discussed the need of receiving a rather substantial sum from each family interested in Bible distribution. We discussed the possibility of most people not being in a position to write a check for ten or twenty dollars, particularly those with large families. We also considered the fact that almost everybody was buying things on the installment plan. The Lord gave us the idea of a bank program. The idea of putting a nickel in the bank every day and a dime on Sunday seemed rather attractive. This could produce $200,000 a year or one million dollars in five years.

The idea was an excellent one, but there remained much to be done. I approached several of my closest friends. Some of them were quite apprehensive. One said, "You're never going to raise a million dollars without a lot of headaches," and I replied, "Very few people have raised such an amount without a headache or two."

During the first year most of the banks were placed by Mr. Ackerman and me. Our staff members were also encouraged to offer these banks. With God's help we spoke at many morning services displaying a bank on the pulpit.

After inspecting many banks, we finally decided on one shaped like the world. Mr. Ackerman, upon my instructions, visited a wholesale toy market in New York City. He looked at scores of banks and finally just the right world bank was discovered. At that time the bank was being manufactured in Puerto Rico. When the man who sold them was asked the cost, he inquired how many were needed. When our director told him 10,000 banks, he stared in disbelief and shook his head.

The World Bank Program met with opposition even among some of our closest friends. Some thought the cost of the world bank, a little over a dollar, was very high, and a few people said, "Why don't they put that money into Bibles?" There was only one thing to do, even though it was a very expensive move. In order to give impetus to this program, my wife and I decided we would donate the first 10,000 banks.

We went to one of the leading Christian magazine publishers of the day. We took the editor to lunch and told him what we had in mind. He smiled, and said, "Well, there are a lot of organizations that talk about raising a million dollars. Come back and see me when you collect the million." We never did go back - not because God didn't give us the million dollars; He gave us more than that! But we soon realized that with the Lord on our side great things could be done, even though a few editors refused to go along with the plan.

At first the bank program was staffed by volunteer help. All collections were made by people interested in the League. However, once the novelty wore off it became difficult to collect through volunteer workers, though to this day we have some very faithful volunteer collectors. Then God gave us an entirely new idea in connection with the World Bank Program. We felt there must be a great number of Christian men, former elders and officers in the church who had reached the age of sixty-five, who would still be willing to be used in the service of God. We decided to set up a program to be called the World Bank Ambassador Program and solicited the services of such men paying a small amount since many of them were on pension.

The caption of an advertisement in one of the religious magazines read, "Life begins at 65." One gentleman wrote, "I just read your ad but I am eight years too old; your advertisement said, 'Life begins at 65' and I am 73." Men were directed to us from all walks of life. The first collector who came to us was Mr. Douwe Tamminga, the man, you may recall, who prayed at my bedside in 1936. He was retired from the International Harvester Company and collected banks until shortly before he went to be with the Lord. He was responsible for bringing in more than $100,000 for the Bibleless homes of the world before the Lord called him home.

Among other collectors were a retired painter, a former real estate man, a lay missionary, a church custodian, a farmer. Although they represented many different backgrounds, all were filled with a desire to do the Lord's will. One of the greatest thrills that I have ever experienced

106

came at a meeting as I listened to these men tell of their experiences. They have gone out in sleet and snow, they have gone from door to door, they have given much spiritual guidance to families who have asked for advice, and meanwhile they have collected substantial amounts for the World Home Bible League's ministry. With excellent supervision represented by such men as Mr. William Brondyk of Muskegon, Michigan, and Mr. Walter Aardsma of Chicago, Illinois, they are instrumental in furnishing a substantial part of the budget of the World Home Bible League's operation each year.

The story of the World Bank Program would not be complete without mentioning the faithful volunteer workers. A woman in Friesland, Wisconsin, collected banks for many years through her local church. Another woman in California also was instrumental in bringing in much revenue from world banks. Other volunteers worked hard and long in the program. Some of these people became almost legendary. Although many years have gone by, many of the bank holders in the eastern part of our country still talk about the volunteer, Mr. William Meines, who so faithfully carried out this charge until his death some years ago.

The program was not without its disappointments but the encouragements far outweighed every disappointing factor. Along the way God gave us many little incidents that we believed to be signposts pointing to the fact that we were on the right road. Let me share a few with you at this time.

AN EXPERIENCE ON A TRAIN

Mr. Ackerman was invited to present the world bank plan for the first time on the east coast. This was about 1952 or 1953. It was decided that he would take along 120 banks. While on the train Mr. Ackerman wondered whether it was wise to offer these banks; maybe after all God didn't want this to be done. What if they were presented and no one came forward to take one? As the wheels of the train clicked on, more and more doubts began to assail; the devil seemed to be extra busy that night.

Then Mr. Ackerman turned to the Lord for some assurance and asked that something might occur to give him confidence that banks would be placed in the East and that the program itself would be successful nation wide. He found it difficult to sleep. Walking to the rear of the car, he went into the men's lounge. A very prosperous-looking man was sitting there puffing on a big cigar. Greetings were exchanged and a conversation began. It turned out that the man was the president of a large bank in New Jersey. Mr. Ackerman asked him how the banking business was and he replied it was quite good but he had had a hard time getting started because he represented the second bank in town. The first bank had been so popular for so many years that people hesitated to change their accounts or start new accounts in his bank. Then the banker said something that startled our director. He said, "You know, what really gave us our big break was a little bank program that we initiated," and he told of purchasing a little bank into which people could put money. It was given to anybody who would deposit a dollar. Thousands of people began saving their nickels and dimes in these little banks and the accounts began to come in and this was one of the ways in which the bank became known and in which thousands of new accounts were started in only nine months.

Mr. Ackerman excused himself, went to his seat, and took the sample world bank from his satchel. He explained the World Bank Program to the bank executive and asked his opinion. The banker reacted warmly and said, "You are on the right track; if you push hard enough there is no doubt at all in my mind that you can raise the million dollars."

Sleep came soon as Mr. Ackerman thought over the strange circumstances. How was it possible that of all the trains running at that time between Chicago and the east coast this particular man would be in this particular car at this particular time and that he would be a banker, a banker who owed a measure of success to a little bank in which people put nickels and dimes?

The next day a meeting was held at Terrace Lake, New Jersey. The new World Bank Program was presented. One hundred and nineteen people came forward for a world bank. As our director was leaving the place - walking on air - a man came up to him and said, "Don't take that bank back to Chicago, I will take it and give it to some family." Exactly 120 banks were placed and today, more than fifteen years later, some of those people who took the banks at that time are still putting in their contributions.

A TERMINAL DISEASE AND AN OBLIGATION

When the first banks were placed in homes we visualized a five-year plan. Later this time limit was discontinued because most people found this such a convenient way of giving that they hardly missed the change and they felt it was a good cause for which they wanted to continue their support.

A woman in a church in Indiana accepted one of the banks on the initial five-year plan. A year later she was informed that she had cancer and had only one year to live. When the collector came to her home she said, "There is one obligation which I must fulfill. I want to raise at least one hundred dollars through this bank before I die. That's what I pledged and that's what I am going to do."

109

And she did!

SACRIFICIAL GIVING

From Boyden, Iowa, came the following testimony given to us by a Christian woman: "My parents became interested in the World Home Bible League in 1950. I remember their joy and excitement as they showed us the little bank that was to collect the gifts to help place Bibles in every home of the world. All of the children, but especially the grandchildren, were invited to share in this great project. It was quite an occasion when the little bank was taken from the shelf and someone would give a gift. The grandchildren particularly were very eager. They needed little encouragement to participate."

It was on December 30, 1950, that Mr. De Wyld went to be with his Lord. The family took an offering to be sent to the World Home Bible League, the project which had been so dear to his heart. The mother decided that the program of placing Bibles in every home throughout the world should continue constantly to challenge them. When they came together for the mother's birthday she requested that no gift be brought to her but as a family they should share in the great work of Bible distribution.

There were many instances, some of them heart-touching, others humorous. God knew there were times when we had to wipe tears from our eyes but He also knew that we needed to smile once in a while.

MORE THAN MONEY

One of our ambassadors found life to be very boring after the death of his beloved wife, but he found a new joy in collecting the little banks. Now he felt he was being used in a particular way for the advancement of the Lord's work on earth. One day he came to our office with a very strange request. He said, "There is a bank in a home which is located outside of my territory, but I would like to have

permission to pick up this bank for personal reasons."
Permission was granted, and about six months later the
man came and asked, "Could I have two weeks off?" We
inquired as to the reason and he explained, "That bank
holder I told you about was Mrs. - and we are going to get
married, and we would like to leave on a little wedding
trip."

WHAT'S MINE IS MINE

Another widow and widower were considering
marriage. They had set the wedding date and had talked
over which house they were going to live in, what they
were going to do with the extra home, etc. Everything
seemed to be set. Then the man became involved in quite a
serious problem so far as he was concerned and said,
"Look, I want to explain something to you. I accepted a
little bank from the World Home Bible League and after
we are married I would like us to put in our contribution
together and send it to the League."

Up to this time everything had been all right but it was
here that the widow objected strenuously. She quickly
pointed out that she too had one of these banks and she
did not intend to give it up. He should give up his bank!
"No," said he, "you should give up your bank." Both of
them were stubborn; he would not give up his bank nor
would she give up her bank. I am happy to report that the
marriage took place and the problem was solved. For many
years this couple had two banks in their home. The two
banks were on the same table, and periodically the League
received two checks, one from the husband and one from
the wife.

WORLD BANKS ARE STILL BEING PLACED TODAY

More than 10,000 families now systematically place
their coins in the banks and as a result millions of people
all over the world have received a copy of the Scripture in

their own language and more than two million dollars has been given. Many of the families who have world banks send their contributions by mail. In addition, at least twenty-five men are engaged in placing and periodically collecting these world banks. Contrary to rumors that occasionally come to us, these men are never paid a commission. They receive a nominal remuneration based on the number of banks in their particular area, but in no instance is any commission paid to any representative of the League for the gathering in of funds.

Ambassadors are men who have been officers in the church and faithful members. The money the League does pay to the men represents a small portion and much of this in turn is usually given to the church in free-will offerings and church assessments. Many, many pages of this book could be filled with stories that emanate from this phase of our activities. Perhaps we could sum it up best by sharing with you a letter which came to me in September 1967.

"Dear Mr. Chapman:

"In a few days I will be 79 years old, but hope and pray our Lord may spare me so that I can keep up this World Bank collecting for another five years. My funds are rather limited now due to circumstances but I am enclosing a $10.00 check above my usual support.

"I count it a privilege to be an ambassador for the World Home Bible League to collect funds for the Bibleless homes and so the missionaries may have Bibles to work with.

"Yesterday I left with banks and materials in hopes of obtaining ten more new contributors. I got twelve. Not bad for an old man, is it?

"Wishing you and yours, Mr. Chapman, our Lord's choicest blessing. I always like to think as long as you and

112

I are here our Lord has a purpose with our life." Signed - John Timmer.

If you have a world bank in your home, I want to thank you on behalf of all the families who have received the Scripture because you are faithful in giving.

If you do not have a world bank in your home, perhaps you ought to write for one today to the World Home Bible League, 16801 Van Dam Road, South Holland, Illinois 60473, and join with more than ten thousand other families in this project of systematic giving for Scripture distribution.

WE BEGAN TO SPEAK IN TONGUES

The League became involved in the distribution of foreign language Scripture when pastors and missionaries asked for materials to be distributed among ethnic groups in our large metropolitan areas. There were also urgent requests for Spanish material to be distributed to migratory workers. Other requests came for French-speaking people in Canada and for large groups of Italian people who had migrated to Canada. Obviously, the most economical way to meet these requests was to buy the Bibles, Testaments, or portions, directly from existing sources. These were the old-line Bible societies of the world. Although this method worked well in early years as the work of the League progressed, there were problems. The League was committed largely to a give-away policy and often the materials available in foreign languages were rather expensive for free distribution. The format of the Scirpture offered at times presented a problem. It became increasingly apparent that if the League were to be an effective Scripture-distribution agency to meet the needs of a variety of language-oriented people, it would sooner or later have to get into the printing, and perhaps into the translation, of foreign language Scripture.

We also received many requests for the translation into foreign languages of our Scripture booklet, *God Speaks.* Within a very short time after its introduction copies of this booklet appeared in Spanish, French, Arabic,

Japanese, Chinese, Portuguese, and Tamil. This, in a strict sense, represented the initial effort that the League made toward translation. Copies were submitted to qualified missionaries in the field and subsequently this material was printed.

Difficulty was encountered when missionaries requested large numbers of Scriptures in a given language and the League discovered that such Scriptures were inevitably copyrighted. Because of copyright restrictions, the League could not produce this material no matter when, where, how, or in what quantity it desired.

As the work of the League became better known and there was more exposure to various missionary endeavors in foreign lands, other problems arose indicating that the League should do something about translation. One of the early examples was the case of the Reverend L. Paul Moore, a United Presbyterian missionary in Africa. For seven years he had been on a translation committee working on the production of the Bulu New Testament. After this work had been completed it was submitted to a committee. The committee, however, was not in favor of publishing the material because of what appeared to be a theological dispute. Meanwhile, the people in the Cameroons were without this New Testament. Through the intercession of a person affiliated with the Back to the Bible Broadcast in Lincoln, Nebraska, officials of the League were called in. After a conference with the missionary, who came to the United States to explain his problem, the League felt the leading of the Lord to publish the Bulu New Testament. This was our first translation of an entire New Testament, and we were on our way. Later we had a request for the publication of a Scripture booklet in Sahu, a language of Eritrea. This Scripture was eventually distributed in that country by a missionary of the Orthodox Presbyterian Church.

The League's intense interest in making available the best possible translation, true to both the original Greek and Hebrew, prompted it to investigate further the activities of the Lockman Foundation in California. This was brought about particularly by the uneasiness of evangelicals in Japan over the publication of a Japanese Scripture. Most of the pastors not affiliated with Japan's national church, the Kyodan, felt that the Japanese version of some texts left much to be desired. The Lockman Foundation, very much concerned over this problem, began to spend vast sums of money to produce the new evangelical Japanese Bible. The League, vitally interested in obtaining such a translation, met with Mr. Dewey Lockman and at that time friendships were cultivated that resulted in the League's using not only the text of the new Japanese Bible, but also using the *New American Standard Version* in the printing of Scripture booklets and a complete New Testament.

For many years the League knew of the activities of Mr. John Beekman, who served the Wycliffe Bible Translators in Mexico. The story of Mr. Beekman's life was recently written in a book published in 1967 by Zondervan, entitled *Peril by Choice*. Mr. Beekman came from Midland Park, New Jersey, where Mr. Ackerman lived as a young man. He also was a member of the Midland Park Reformed Church, of which the Reverend Gordon Van Oostenburg was pastor. The lines, therefore, were quite closely drawn. We visited Mr. Beekman many times in our trips to Mexico.

In 1960, Wycliffe Bible personnel, serving with the Summer Institute of Linguistics in the South Sea Islands, began to inquire of the World Home Bible League whether it was interested in publishing Scripture in the dialect of some of the South Sea Islanders. Guhu-Samane was the first dialect in which the League printed a new translation developed by Wycliffe Bible personnel. Several other publications in South Sea Island dialects followed.

There were several factors God seemed to use to draw together the ministries of the Wycliffe Bible Translators and the World Home Bible League. Both were committed to the presentation of the Gospel to every living creature through the written Word. Because of this commitment, Wycliffe personnel were zealously engaged in the translation of the Word, and World Home Bible League personnel were busy in the publication and distribution. Copyrights restricted the full orbit of distribution of a Gospel or a New Testament, or even the use of such text, in diglot versions or monoglot. Both agencies realized that the Holy Scripture was written with the intention of revealing the person and work of the Lord Jesus Christ. Therefore, the Bible, or a portion of it, represented a weapon for spiritual warfare. If there were only 100 believers in a tribe of 100,000 Indians, it would seem ridiculous to print a very small edition of the Scripture as there would be no sale to anyone other than the believers. Why not, argued the League, publish Scripture so that unbelievers would be exposed to it also? Forget that sales were necessary and, wherever possible, try to get a portion of the Scripture into the hands of men and women regardless of whether or not they paid for it.

It was on November 7, 1968, that the World Home Bible League assumed a major responsibility in relation to Wycliffe Bible translations for Mexico and South America. It was estimated at that time that the League would be involved in more than $122,000 worth of publications for Wycliffe over a two-year period.

The Wycliffe organization and its translators are

117

responsible for bringing the Scripture to the point of publication. Then the League takes over and assumes the publishing cost.

Once again, in faith, believing that this was a worthy project and a work in which God would have us busy, we accepted the challenge. A commentary on the work of the World Home Bible League in conjunction with the Wycliffe Bible Translators is found in the following letter written to us by Mr. John Beekman:

December 26, 1968

World Home Bible League
425 W. 107th St.
Chicago, Illinois 60628

Dear Christian Friends:

The Wycliffe Bible Translators, Inc. is an organization dedicated to the task of translating God's Word into the various languages of the world. While our missionaries hold literacy classes, engage in medical work, attend linguistic conferences, and conduct institutes on linguistics at three university campuses in the United States and also in Australia, Britain, Germany, and New Zealand, the primary goal of the organization is to provide the Scriptures in written form for the various aboriginal groups of the world as a means of winning converts who will establish strong, indigenous churches.

The Wycliffe Bible translators are working in over 420 different languages in Alaska, Australia, Bolivia, Brazil, Canada, Guatemala, Honduras, Colombia, Ecuador, India, Nepal, Mexico, New Guinea, the United States, Peru, The Philippines, Surinam, Vietnam, Ghana, and Nigeria. The translator pioneers in areas where other missionaries have not been assigned. In areas where missionaries are already

118

assigned to establish a church, the Wycliffe translators work in cooperation with them. This can best be illustrated with the work in Mexico among the Chols and Tzeltal Indians where Wycliffe produced the respective New Testaments and more recent missionary arrivals are now living among these Indians and guiding in the development of the church.

In each country where we have allocated missionary-translators, we have also provided linguistic, literacy, and translation consultants, most of whom have either a Master's degree or a Ph.D. This assures a standard quality control of all the work which is produced by the membership. All translations are checked carefully as to the accuracy and effectiveness of the alphabet selected, the grammar used, and the choice of words made, in order to determine where the translation needs improvement from the standpoint of readability and intelligibility. A verse-by-verse check is also made with a native speaker present to determine the exegetical faithfulness of the translation to the original. Generally, a translation passes through two or three revisions before it is finally published. When one considers the gigantic task of publishing 420 New Testaments within the next twenty years, plus additional ones where tribal groups are still awaiting a missionary-translator to accept the challenge of preparing a translation for the entrance of the gospel light, one can understand the deep gratitude which the Wycliffe Bible Translators have for the ministry of the World Home Bible League. They have accepted the major responsibility for the publication of New Testaments and portions in Mexico. At the same time, they will continue to help in the publication program of Scripture materials for other countries in which Wycliffe works. We appreciate the World Home Bible League and those associated with them who are making possible the provision of God's Word to the more than two thousand tribal groups still without any portion of God's Word. As never before there is an accelerated activity in the translation of Scriptures for the peoples of the world. Your interest in promoting and helping in this Spirit-directed movement is much appreciated.

Sincerely yours in Him,
John Beekman
Corporation Translation Coordinator

On ˙November 1, 1969, the Wycliffe organization offered a wider choice of translations to be published. These involved not only Latin America, but the Philippine Islands, and Vietnam. The World Home Bible League, together with the New York Bible Society, formed an organization known as "Scriptures Unlimited." Through this organization, directed by Board members of each of the parent organizations and its directors, twice the number of translations originally published are contemplated.

The Reverend John Van Harn, William Chapman, William Ackerman, and other staff members, called on more than forty pastors. They explained the project and asked whether they would take this matter up with their church boards for approval. Not one of the pastors turned us down. The response was very gratifying and money is beginning to come in to support this project. Now the League intends to begin working in other areas on tribal dialects in North America.

Many other evangelicals who witnessed the progress of the ministry of the World Home Bible League were eager to have a part and God directed them to help us. Ken Taylor of the Tyndale House Foundation was one of them.

He offered the use of *The Living Series* text in a missionary edition. Fifty thousand of these were sent to Vietnam. Over 200,000 booklets in *The Living Series* text were published for special occasions such as Easter and Christmas. We owe a deep vote of gratitude to Mr. Lockman and the Lockman Foundation, and to Mr. Taylor and Tyndale House Foundation for the wonderful spirit of sharing they have displayed to us. All the Scripture the League has published in these particular texts has been done without recourse to royalty. In other words, the use of the text was given free to the World Home Bible League. The League was given permission to publish in almost any quantity or format the text of these translations and paraphrases.

If permission to use texts that freely had been given to the League in the beginning by existing Bible societies, perhaps there would not have been a need for the League to enter into these areas. However, we believe now, looking back, that God led and that this was His idea and not ours. The reason for our conviction lies in the area of His apparent stamp of approval in giving us loyal friends who not only released to us texts that originally cost them a very large amount of money, but also in giving us a great number of pastors and church workers who put their shoulders to the wheel to help us share the cost of translation. This to us was God's nod of approval and man's vote of confidence in what had transpired.

Yes, the ministry of the World Home Bible League is a saga of God's moving in a distinct and formidable way in all that we tried to do for Him. Because God is timeless His message also is timeless. The distribution of the Word of God through the World Home Bible League could include many more pages of interesting material. Even as this book goes to press, new developments occur in our Bible

121

correspondence department, Bible translation and the distribution of contemporary editions of the Scripture. Challenging and daring new fields are opening for distribution every year. It seems that God is writing a new chapter every few weeks. The eternal results of the distribution of the Word of God are dependent only upon the promise He made in Isaiah 55:11, "My word...shall not return unto me void..." Only in eternity will the full story be known. This is only a very small part of it and that is the reason for the title of this book, *Story Without an End.*

SHEAVES

As the Scripture was distributed and men, women, and children began to read it, the Holy Spirit prepared the hearts of many to receive its truth. This was of great inspiration to us and many reports were received of souls saved. When the ministry experienced disappointments and the road was rough these were the signposts that kept us going. We realized that even if one soul were saved it was of more value than all the wealth of the world. We were also impressed by the fact that the Word of God knew no particular geographical limitation or cultural background. It spoke to men in Cuba, in Europe, in the Orient, and all over the world. The Word is no respecter of persons for the magnetism of the word generated by the Holy Spirit draws God's ransomed own to Him wherever they are. Among the reports of conversions that came to us were the following:

THERE IS ONLY ONE GOD

In one of the small towns in the center of the island of Cuba a woman stood up to testify at a church service. She said that about three years had passed since she had received a Spanish New Testament and had begun to read it. When some of her friends discovered her new pastime they warned her that if she continued to read the book she most certainly would lose her mind. But somehow or other the book had a strange fascination and attraction for her. The more she read it, the more she wanted to read it. Even the local priest emphatically stated that she would go "loco" if she continued to read the forbidden volume. But she persisted and one day suddenly the full light of the Gospel's meaning shown upon her pathway.

With a radiant expression of joy on her face she stood up to testify at the church meeting. She held the little red Testament high over her head and gave her testimony. She concluded by stating, "And now I know there is only one God because I found Him between the covers of this little book."

FIRST FRUITS

One day a truck driver backed his truck alongside our office. While we were assisting in unloading, he asked, "What's in these boxes?"

I informed him, "Bibles."

He exclaimed, "This entire truckload is all Bibles!"

I answered, "14,000 or more of them."

He continued to move the boxes to the rear of the truck as helpers were bringing them into the office. Then he asked, "What do you do with these Bibles? Do you sell them?"

"No, we give them away," I explained.

"To whom?" he asked.

"To men like you," I told him.

"Why?" he queried.

"Because we are thankful to God for a saving knowledge of Jesus Christ. We are grateful to Him Who shed His blood on Calvary's cross. You, too, can have that hope; you can't buy it; you can't merit it - it is the gift of God," I said.

"Speaking of Bibles reminds me that I have been a bad boy," he admitted.

We spoke of the Bible as being powerful, quick and sharper than any two-edged sword. These Bibles were still

124

on the truck, in the cartons, but God had already used their message to convict this man of sin in his past life.

Later we spoke further about sin and the price paid for sin on Calvary's cross. He accepted a Bible and promised to read it, and as tears trickled down his face, he said, "This may be the most important delivery that I have ever made in my life." There are many people like that truck driver in your community, in your city. We want to reach them and we challenge you to seek them.

IF THE SON SHALL MAKE YOU FREE

During the Castro revolution in Cuba scores of pastors from one end of the island to the other testified of the power of the Word of God to transform men. Many of these testimonies involved the lives of men and women condemned to die. A pastor told of one of President Batista's followers who was quilty, by his own admission, of killing more than twenty Cuban people. He was given a World Home Bible League Testament. He read it over and over again. Early in the morning of the day he died he walked before a firing squad with his little Testament in hand and gave a brief testimony of his newly-found confidence and belief in Jesus Christ. His last request was to die, not standing up, but on his knees praying. He did so and he held the little Testament high. A missionary reported, "The rifles cracked, his body fell backward into the ditch, but I am sure his soul sprang up to heaven."

"If the Son therefore shall make you free, ye shall be free indeed." (John 8:36).

SOMETHING BAD WILL HAPPEN!

A girl received one of our red Spanish Testaments. She became very interested in its message. She was warned by the church authorities to discontinue reading it because if she did read it, some bad things would happen in her life. She ignored these warnings and eventually the Holy Spirit

125

moved in her heart to accept the truth of what she read.

Her entire family were of a different faith and discouraged her in her new-found faith. The children in school continued to tell her that something bad would happen to her for forsaking the mother church for the religion of the Evangelicals. Then it did happen. The girl was sitting on the tailboard of her father's pickup truck. The truck suddenly started up and she toppled off, hitting her head on the pavement. She was rushed to the hospital and it was revealed that she had a brain concussion. The visitors from her former church stopped in to warn her that this was the direct result of changing her faith. The children at school said this was a lesson for Marietta - this is what she could expect for becoming an Evangelical. For a time it appeared that the tremendous pressure put on this young girl would cause her to give up her faith.

But the Lord intervened. About a month later she was released from the hospital. She was able to testify to friends that her faith was now stronger than it had ever been before.

THE MAN ON CRUTCHES

At a church service in Warren, Ohio, the pastor turned to me and asked, "Do you see that man with the crutches making his way into the back pew? That man lived near this church, almost right next to the parsonage, for sixteen years. On several occasions I heard him cursing and he claimed to be an infidel. In recent months he was taken seriously ill and I was able to get into the home to visit him. He failed to respond to my kindness and was belligerent on his sickbed. Finally, in desperation I said, 'If you will not listen to me, at least listen to the message of this book,' and I left one of your Bibles with him and walked out of his home. Our family was much in prayer that God would use the Word to convict this man of sin

126

and turn him to the Lamb of God. God answered that prayer in a remarkable manner. Publicly he has taken a stand for Christ. Tonight his wife is with him in the service. This is the first time she has ever attended this church."

A HINDU CONVERT

We received a report in our office concerning a Hindu convert in India who could neither read nor write. Others read the Bible to him. John 1:12 eventually became his favorite text. It reads in part, "But as many as received him, to them gave he power to become the sons of God..."

"I have received Christ," said the Hindu, "so I have become a son of God." He went back into the village where he lived and was so radiantly happy that he kept repeating over and over again, "I have become a son of God." His life was so transformed and his simple witness was so effective that many of the villagers also wanted to become sons of God.

This convert was said to have won many of the village for Christ. He was just a poor illiterate Hindu who realized that he had indeed become a son of God. Because he longed for others to become sons of God also, the Holy Spirit used him in this simple yet remarkable way.

THE POWER OF THE WORD (JULY 1944)

A grateful missionary related the following:

"Fifty-five years ago a Roman Catholic, whom I knew in my native Italy, was converted to the Presbyterian Church. He came to my new home in Mt. Vernon, New York, and gave me a copy of the Bible in the Italian language. He asked me to read the third and fourth chapters of the Gospel of John.

"He also invited me to visit him in the Bloomfield (New Jersey) Presbyterian Seminary. After several days I went and after a short conversation he took me to his room and

127

there asked me, 'Pasquale, would you like to know how the Protestants pray?'

"I said, 'Yes, I would.' I used to love to pray when I was in the Catholic church. My prayers were both in Latin and Italian, which we were obliged to read.

"So we knelt down and he prayed. I was very much impressed by his oral prayer. We arose and again he asked me as I departed to read the third and fourth chapters of the Gospel of John. He made me promise that and I did. When I got home that evening after ten o'clock, I went to my humble study and read those two chapters. As I began to read I felt some power over me. I felt different and as I continued in prayer I burst into tears and asked God to forgive my sins.

"Then and there I became a new man. I have never forgotten it, and I asked God as I prayed in Italian to open the way for me to preach the Gospel of Jesus Christ to the Italians in America.

"This is my short story. I hope and pray that God may use this testimony as you publish it for the glory of Jesus Christ as the Saviour, the Lord, the Redeemer and Friend of man.

"I have the highest regard for you and the great work which you are doing by spreading the Holy Bible in America."

A NEW ANDREW BY FIRE

John and Clarence Van Ens told us the following story: They could see it, but they could hardly believe it!

There was dense smoke and the stench of burning cloth rising from the bonfire near the parsonage of a church in Dehiwala, Ceylon. A tall American pastor, his wife, and a small group of Ceylonese men stood watching as the flames poked through gaps in the heap of orange clothing - the robes of a Buddhist priest - on the evening of October

128

19, 1962.

Rev. Clarence Van Ens and the lay evangelists of the church were probably grateful that the smoke gave them a chance to rub their eyes without embarrasment. They were deeply moved, for one of the group around the fire would certainly be persecuted and possibly killed for committing this act! He had convinced them that he wished to belong to Jesus Christ alone and no longer follow the Buddha.

Months before, the old Andrew had been watching a Christian missionary passing out literature in his village and he sent a small boy to fetch him a sample to satisfy his curiosity. It would have been quite improper for him in his orange robe to request one personally.

He read and was intrigued. There was an address on the piece and he wrote for more. Because someone in Canada or the United States, In God's providence, had recognized the need for Bibles in the homes of the world and had sent a part of the substance God entrusted to him to the World Home Bible League, it was possible for the Ceylon Home Bible League to send him a copy of the Gospel of John. Later a Bible correspondence course was also sent to him.

In spite of the resistance of his senior priest, he studied the Scripture. Eventually he sought out the lay evangelists of the Dehiwala Church and declared his interest in and then his acceptance of the Gospel. In October he left the temple for good.

TO LIVE A LONG TIME

"I was walking on the street in Chichibu when I first met Inoue-san in September, 1961," wrote Rev. Maas Vander Bilt, missionary from Japan.

"We fell into animated conversation and found that we lived close to each other. I invited him to my house and he invited me to his.

"I was the first to accept the invitation and found him

in his nine-by-twelve shack. His family was six or eight birds. He sleeps in one corner of the room on a platform a foot and a half from the floor covered with a tatami mat. In another corner he cooks - we shall say no more about that! The rest of the room was filled with treasures, it seemed, of a human pack rat. It came out that Inoue-san received a bit of financial help from the city welfare agency but for the rest he collected junk and garbage and did odd jobs. I asked whether he would consider picking up our garbage for 50c a week. He said he would if he could come twice a week. The deal we made then has never been broken - it has developed into one of the fondest of personal relationships.

"When Inoue-san came to my house, I gave him a World Home Bible League New Testament. He had never seen a Bible before, so I spent half an hour explaining it to him. I remember distinctly his reaction to John 3:16: 'Nagai aida ikiru koto ga dekimasu, ne,' he exclaimed. ('Man, a person can live for a long time!')

"From time to time I would talk to Inoue-san as he came faithfully on Monday and Thursday to pick up the garbage. I knew he was reading the New Testament because he would ask me questions about many things we had not talked about. He seemed to learn and believe.

"In April, 1962, we held our city-wide evangelistic campaign. I worked things out so Inoue-san would have a front-row seat where he would be able to hear well. The Lord moved his heart as Koji Honda, Japan's most zealous evangelist, preached, and when the invitation was given Inoue-san quickly went to the front. Evangelist Honda took time to talk with him personally, and that night he believed in his Lord publicly.

"Inoue-san is now 76 years old. He is a cheerful old man, content with his lot. His wife is dead and his children more or less ignore him. He still keeps busy with his little jobs, but also he now often comes to church. That Inoue-san believes Christ, I have no doubt. Of course, the many years in paganism have formed deep habits which are not easily broken, but I believe the Lord is smiling upon this broken vessel and I work in the high hope that his name is written in heaven."

A missionary's love, a World Home Bible League New Testament, an evangelist's preaching - all used by God to make an aged Japanese garbage collector not only know, but even experience - "Man, a person can live for a long time!"

SOWING ALONG THE ROADSIDE (APRIL 1949)

The Lord leads in mysterious ways His wonders to perform. As I was returning home one dark, rainy evening after a day of calling on farm folk in hill and dale, the headlights of the car suddenly revealed a jeep stalled in the road. A lad was trying to push it. I stopped to see whether I could help. The lad asked if I would tow the jeep a short distance as the wires were wet. Although it was quite a load for a light Ford V-8, I reasoned that I could probably get him to a main road about a mile or so down the road. However, near the top of a sharp grade the wheels began to spin. I kept praying and finally we made it to the top. By the time we reached the bottom of the hill the engine of the jeep had dried and began running. As the lad turned to thank me, I had the opportunity to question him regarding his spiritual condition. He said that he had come a long distance to bale hay, but had experienced nothing but trouble. He had taken the job of baling hay to get away from problems of another job, and it seemed that everything was against him. I told him then of Jesus' hardships in his behalf, of God's love, of the way of salvation. He accepted the Lord as his Saviour almost immediately, for his heart undoubtedly had been prepared by the Spirit of God.

After a bit of counsel on Christian living, the young man told me that he had no Bible but would like one and would read it. After entering a record of his decision and the date in the front, I presented to him an American Home Bible League Bible. We went carefully through the auxiliary page in the flyleaf of the Bible, underlined a few verses of Scripture, and then had prayer together. Then he told me how an unseen force seemed to have driven him from his home to this place and then even to where he had been stalled in the jeep right in the middle of the road. He said he believed it had been God leading him to salvation, and so do I.

A sower, Chicago, Illinois

TRANS WORLD MISSIONS

A letter received from the founder of Trans World Missions, formerly the Airmail from God Mission, the Reverend Nyles Huffman, who has since gone to be with the Lord, was a source of great encouragement to us.

"When Brother Chapman visited with our group here in Mexico he went on a trip into Guerrero to a little village called Teloloapan. After the service Brother Chapman personally handed World Home Bible League Testaments to the people. Two years later a group of us stopped in this village to make a trip to a village on the other side of a huge mountain directly behind Teloloapan. We stopped at a humble hut; we noticed evangelical literature, and a little red World Home Bible League Testament that had been read much but carefully handled. When we inquired about these things, Raoul, the owner of the home, told us that he had been saved through the Testament that was given to him one night after a service. Since then he had started a Sunday school class in his home and was going to nearby villages winning others to the Lord. This Testament was given to him by your own beloved Mr. Chapman. We took Raoul with us over the mountain to the other village so that he could gain experience from hearing and seeing our native evangelist, Roque, hold a service. Raoul was greatly encouraged by our visit and is still busy in this area winning souls.

"Our Evangelist Roque said, 'With great joy people in the town of Jarip, Guerrero, received God's written Word for the first time in their lives when after an evangelistic service I handed them New Testaments.' First the Testaments were presented with much typical Mexican ceremony to the president and other officials of the town, and then to the other people. Don Roque said, 'With my own eyes I saw three persons down at the edge of the crowd, with their oil candles beside them for light, start reading. As they read and discussed what they were reading, their eyes shone with approval of what they were reading in God's Word as they nodded their heads in agreement.' "

HOSTILITY

"In the village of Viastancia, Michoacan, the next day, I spoke to the authorities and asked them if we could present to them and to the village people a sacred Book, the Word of God. They gave me permission and called all the people together. Before an assembly of about 350 of the townsfolk, we presented the sacred Book to the president and told him it was the Word of God. We explained, 'This Book teaches the plan of salvation and the remedy that God has given for sin. It also contains the promises that God has for all those who want to accept Him in their heart.' After I talked to them and showed a film by flashlight projector, we asked how many would like to accept Christ as Saviour. They all raised their hands.

We could see in their shining faces the joy in their hearts. After again presenting the authorities with the Word, we gave Testaments to the villagers who promised to read them. The next morning the missionary group had a big surprise. They saw the priest going from house to house scolding the people for taking the Testaments. He came close to the place where we were. We saw that when the priest tried to grab a Testament from one of the men the man hugged the Book close to him with both arms and wouldn't let go of it. He shouted, 'You have never spoken to us of what is in this Book, and it is good. I am keeping mine.' "

THE BROKEN IDOL

"In the State of Oaxaca, we went into some villages way out from nowhere, and held services and gave Testaments to the people. The presidents were 'proud as peacocks' of theirs and so were the people, but when the priest came to town a couple of weeks later he told the people to destroy them. An idol in front of the church had been broken, and since no one would own up to having broken it he blamed the people who had received Testaments, - practically everyone in town. When the children, especially, wouldn't give up their Testaments, they were ordered beaten.

SOWING IN MANY FIELDS

"We started giving Testaments to the people on the evangelistic trips we made on foot into villages that had previously received the Word dropped by our airplane. Then when we started our correspondence course we began sending Testaments to our graduates along with their certificates.

"In our labors of many years here on the Mexican field, we have found through extensive research that there is nothing so effective as the printed Word of God placed effectively in the hands of the Mexican farmer. To date, we have covered over one-third of the entire Republic of Mexico. Whole communities are feeling the impact of the presence of God.

"Your prayers continually break through the chains of darkness and make the way possible for the Word to reach this darkened land. Only last week the Chief of Customs for the northern region who has recently accepted the Lord, started dropping Gospels for us on Saturdays and Sundays. He was trained by the U.S. Air Force and is an active captain, pilot, and squadron commander in the Mexican Air Force.

"Truly this is the hour for Mexico. We thank you for the encouragement of the World Home Bible League throughout the years. Pray with us and for us as we continue to launch out into larger fields."

Rev. Nyles Huffman

PARTNERS THROUGH PRAYERS AND GIFTS

Throughout this book are recorded many incidents of people committed to the World Home Bible League's ministry. Some of them went to the uttermost parts of the world to distribute the Scripture and to witness concerning the Saviour. It would be difficult to determine just who made the greatest contribution of all, but certainly among the outstanding contributions were those made through prayer.

The tendency also is to count the large gifts, the substantial checks that come in from businessmen, but there are also the little gifts that come from people with great vision. In this chapter are incidents relating prayers that have been offered for our ministry and gifts that have been made by people who have encouraged us tremendously along the way.

MORE PRAYER WARRIORS JOIN US

In 1951 an idea came to many of us vitally interested in the program of the League. There seemed to be a strong feeling that a League prayer meeting should be held each week at a designated time. This meeting would afford an opportunity for all those interested in Scripture distribution to gather and intercede both for those who sow the seed and for those who receive the Scripture. However, it was quite difficult to find a time satisfactory to all. This problem was solved in a unique manner. I suggested to the men that it should be held at a time when everyone who really meant business could be there, but to find such a time seemed an almost impossible task. To make sure that all of us could be there without an excuse, 3:00 A.M. on Monday was suggested. The men began to murmur and complain, but they were reminded that if they were going fishing or leaving on vacation they would get up at that time.

Finally, a compromise was made and we decided to meet at 7:30 A.M. on Monday. It is all right to compromise, you know, if we don't sacrifice our principles. Since 1951 the meetings have been held every Monday morning at 7:30 A.M. - first in Chicago and now in South Holland.

Countless individuals pray for us all over the U.S.A., Canada, and the world. We are always in need of prayer warriors. We invite you to join us as we gather around the throne of God to petition Him for divine direction in this ministry.

In Psalm 65:2 we read, "O thou that hearest prayer." God proves that He is that prayer-hearing God, but He is a prayer-answering God also, for in Psalm 91:15 we read, "He shall call upon me, and I will answer him." We have experienced this over and over again as a result of the Monday morning prayer meeting. We look to Him for many more great things, for He has invited us to "Call unto me, and I will answer thee, and shew thee great and mighty things, which thou knowest no " (Jeremiah 33:3).

God has led us to prayer warriors in many strange places which has been very encouraging. Mr. Evers and I were making calls at a local old people's home one day. During the last visit an interview took place which made an indelible impression upon me. We were in the room of an elderly lady. She spoke to us in her frail voice and testified, "I cannot get out of this room any more, but

137

every morning one or two other ladies join me here and we pray together as you distribute the Bible in the languages of the people across the world. We pray that the Lord will bless and that the Scripture will be opened and the cross of Christ will stand forth on its pages. We pray too that the Holy Spirit will convict evil men of sin and turn them to Jesus who takes away the sin of the world."

Early in the history of the American Home Bible League an invitation came to address a Christian businessmen's club which met at the Chicago Athletic Club. On the appointed day I walked around the building several times, finally getting into the elevator. It stopped at the 19th floor. It was here that the meeting was to take place and the chairman met me and asked, "Have you ever spoken here before?"

"No," I replied, "and it is with considerable reluctance that I am here at all because of my lack of experience in addressing groups such as yours."

The chairman put his arm around my shoulder and pointed to a distant door. The door was open and men were coming into the room. The chairman explained that they had just come out of a prayer meeting where they had been on their knees. He looked at me and said, "They were praying for you."

This was a new and thrilling experience. It gave assurance of having been lifted up on the wings of prayer. Never before was such freedom of expression felt. The benefits of that meeting were to be realized throughout many years, as evidenced by some who later supported us as a result of the burdens laid during that presentation.

A PRAYER PARTNER IN A WHEEL CHAIR

An invalid lady was pushed up to the speaker's table in a wheel chair after a League banquet in Canada and said, "You must often become discouraged in your work, but I want you to know that wherever you are at 11:00 o'clock in the morning, Toronto time, this little old lady is praying for you and will pray that you will be given courage, that you will be bold, and that you may have a source of strength surge through your heart and life. I pray that God will enable you to carry on your objective in reaching our generation for Christ.''

PRAYER AND A DOLLAR BILL

A woman brought a gift to our League office one day. She said, "Mr. Chapman, I always pray for the American Home Bible League and for you as you carry on this ministry. It is a good work. I am bringing you my gift. I would like you to use it."

The gift was only one dollar. It would have been much easier for me to give this lady five dollars than to take her one dollar, but I knew that would not have been right. She displayed dedicated, consecrated giving. I accepted it, then turned to the lady and asked, "Let's see what we can do with your gift, shall we?" As I picked up five Testaments, I explained that we could send one to Spain, one to Mexico, one to Cuba, one to Brazil, and one we could give to a migrant worker right here in the United States.

She exclaimed, "Oh, my, I am a missionary now all over the world."

She stated a great truth; that is exactly what she was, a missionary all over the world. At that time we were paying twenty cents for each Testament. Think of what she accomplished with one dollar invested in Bible distribution. Today the cost of that same Testament is still lower, despite rising costs, thanks to the volunteer workers who are putting together Gospel portions and complete New Testaments. Almost anyone can be a missionary all over the world.

As the Scripture was distributed and as testimonies

came in, enthusiastic reports were received as the work grew. God also inclined the hearts of people to give, and how true it is that God moves in mysterious ways His wonders to perform, for it seemed as if He touched many people in many mysterious and interesting ways. The following are just a few:

A GIFT FROM AN OLD LADY (APRIL 1949)

"I am writing this for a very dear old lady who is eighty-nine years old. She has asked me to tell that your work is a wonderful work. In all her eighty-nine years she says she has never heard of such a wonderful thing. She wants to be a member of the American Home Bible League and will send in her donation from time to time."

A friend

A GIFT FROM A DRUNKARD (APRIL 1949)

"I enclose one dollar from a Belgian to whom I gave a Bible. That man was, humanly speaking, an incurable drunkard. His children had urged his wife to live elsewhere because she was a heart patient and could not live with him any longer. I prayed with him and for him. Later he accepted Christ and is no longer drinking. The children and his wife have begun to have faith in the change which has taken place in his life, and they will soon come back to live with him."

A Christian brother

A BOY AND HIS DUCKS (APRIL 1948)

Marion and Derold De Kock, ages ten and seven, were a couple of real farm lads from Hawarden, Iowa. They raised ducks on their daddy's farm. Many years ago they sold their flock and from the proceeds sent in some money as their membership contribution to the American Home Bible League. In addition to being real farmers, these boys planted the Word of God in our beloved country as spiritual sowers of the Gospel.

140

BOBBY THE NEWSBOY GIVES

Bobby Meerdink was a newspaper carrier in Hull, Iowa, which netted him something over a dollar a week. Challenged with the work of the League, Bobby said he wanted to be a member. Not only was he going to make an initial contribution, but he decided to take a part of his earnings (far exceeding a tithe) to make a regular monthly contribution. Bobby walked the streets carrying his morning papers, but at the same time he carries far better news, the good news of the Gospel to villages of America through his membership in the League.

A TRUE LOVE OFFERING

"A collection was taken among the pupils of the Roseland Christian School on Valentine's Day for the American Home Bible League. Valentines were discouraged and your project was encouraged. We teachers are happy to present to your cause $45.25; prayer accompanies the gift for your cause."

William Brouwer, Principal
Roseland Christian School
Chicago, Illinois

SOME NEW DEVELOPMENTS

One of the most difficult tasks confronting us in the writing of this book is to say finally, "This is the end." And that's exactly the reason this book has the strange title, *Story Without An End*. Each new month something new and exciting occurs and the Lord opens new avenues of service.

BIBLE CORRESPONDENCE DEPARTMENT

A new Bible Correspondence Department, under the supervision of the Rev. John De Vries, has already been widely acclaimed. Churches from the U.S.A., Canada, Great Britain, Australia, India, Pakistan, Ethiopia, and Argentina have ordered this Bible study material. Over 1500 churches and missions are already involved. In a little over a year, approximately 180,000 sections of the Bible study course were distributed by the churches.

Other related programs such as the Bible memory course and a youth program call TIME (Teenagers in Meaningful Evangelism) have been started. The placement of a Gospel in the paraphrased "Reach Out" edition is also being used to introduce the Bible correspondence course to transients, those who are in hotels, motels, railroad stations, airports, etc.

More interesting programs along this line are being contemplated and experimented with in an effort to get people to distribute the Word and to study the Bible.

This advertisement appeared in the Asian edition of the Reader's Digest published during 1970. Three months after it appeared, more than 600 inquiries were received. The cost of this ad was underwritten by the Holland-Zeeland Women's Division of the World Home Bible League.

Why is the Bible the world's best-seller?

Because this unique book is and has been for years and years, the most widely read book in the world.

You may have read the Bible—but have you discovered how exciting and stimulating it can be?

Let us help you with an interesting, systematic, easy, completely FREE plan you can do in your leisure moments, in your home.

Send for our **FREE** Bible Correspondence Course today. Write to B.C.C., Post Box No. 656, Bombay-1 or fill in the coupon below.

To B.C.C., Post Box No. 656, Bombay-1 (Dept:HW)
Please send me your FREE Bible Correspondence Course.

Name..

Address ....

Creative Workshop EBE1   135

THE REV. CHESTER SCHEMPER

The Rev. Chester Schemper, who very early in the history of the League began distributing Scripture among Mexican migratory workers in the Borculo, Michigan, area, became translation coordinator for the League on January 1, 1970. On special loan to the League by the Christian Reformed Board of Missions, Rev. Schemper will occupy this important position.

In this connection he will supervise the translation of the new Spanish Scripture contemplated for completion some time in 1973.

SCRIPTURES UNLIMITED

On November 1, 1969, the World Home Bible League joined hands with the New York Bible Society in a special effort to reach Latin America with the Word.

This is a three-pronged program involving (1) the new vernacular translation of the Spanish Scriptures; (2) the underwriting of publications for the tribal languages of South America as prepared by Wycliffe Bible Translators; and (3) a distribution of over five and one-half million Scirptures for 1970.

CHURCH RELATIONS DIRECTOR

The Rev. John Van Harn, who was on the Advisory Council Board of the World Home Bible League for a number of years, and whose wife serves as president of the National Women's Division, came with the League on a full-time basis effective February 15, 1970. Rev. Van Harn will be responsible for raising funds for the World Home Bible League's share in Scriptures Unlimited and will serve in the capacity of church relations director.

CHILDREN'S BIBLE CRUSADE

In 1965, the Rev. Nicholas Vogelzang, a pastor in La_sing, Illinois, was displeased with the idea of having his children call on homes for "trick or treat" at Halloween

144

time and decided to do something about it. He suggested that, as this was close to Reformation Day, it would be an ideal time to encourage children to accept donations for the World Home Bible League. After all, he reasoned, this was the time when the church commemorated what Martin Luther had done, and Martin Luther was a man who desired to have the Bible in the hands of every person.

The children of the church were receptive to the idea and in the first year, $186 was collected by the boys and girls. In 1966, the project caught on; two additional churches responded and $406 was contributed. In 1967, seven participating churches collected $1,000 for Bible distribution. It was then that Mr. Jacob Porter, of Lansing, Illinois, decided to promote this in a more ambitious way. Programs were presented in churches in Chicago, Oak Park, Wheaton, and Fulton, Illinois; and De Motte, South Bend, and Goshen, Indiana. Interest was high. The program is also being developed in Colorado, Iowa, Minnesota, and Michigan.

The Children's Bible Crusade is the newest fund-raising program developed by the World Home Bible League.

PERSONALIZED SCRIPTURE

One of the most interesting developments in the League's Scripture distribution program throughout the United States and Canada during 1967 was the introduction of World Home Bible League personalized Scripture.

The League contracts for the printing of hundreds of thousands of completed pages of the New Testament and the Gospel of John, and for copies of Scripture compilations. These are delivered to us unbound. We then print special covers for churches which personalize the Scripture so that churches can use them effectively in such situations as house-to-house canvassing, introduction of a

145

church to a new community, or witnessing by the church at specific functions, such as a state fair, etc.

Since the release of this project, more than 100 churches have used personalized Scripture. The imagination of the pastors and promotional committees in the churches surpassed our fondest expectations. Almost all of these churches featured a photo of their church on the front cover, their hour of worship, and an invitation to attend divine services. Others have included the church covenant or doctrinal statement. Clever titles have been introduced. An example is the familiar League publication, *Behold the Answer* which, when used by a group of Canadian churches, was entitled, *100 Questions on Canada's 100th Anniversary*. In South Holland, Illinois, in observance of the Tulip Festival, more than 2,000 booklets with a suitable "tulip time" sketch were presented as souvenirs to be taken home and read. Other ideas ranged from covers depicting the skyline of Chicago, a man with a plow for a plowman's contest in Canada, and a fisherman standing in a stream for a church that ministers to vacationers.

Churches representing the following denominations were involved in special personalized Scripture during the past year: Southern Baptist, Independent Bible Churches, Fellowship Bible Churches of Canada, Evangelical Free Church, the Reformed Church in America, and the Christian Reformed Church. Many other interesting personalized Scripture distribution projects are being planned at the present time.

CHRISTIAN REFORMED LAYMEN'S GROUP (1969-70)

The Christian Reformed Laymen's group of Grand Rapids, Michigan, whose president is Mr. Bob Plekker, in cooperation with the League, has gone into a very extensive Scripture placement program in Mexico. It has

146

set a goal to raise more than $75,000 for this work through radio marathons under the supervision of Mr. Willis Timmer. The peninsula-wide canvass of Yucatan involving Scripture distribution has been launched.

These programs have progressed since this manuscript was submitted to our publisher. We ask you to pray with us that, as each new field opens, God will give us a vision so that we may add with His help many new chapters to the *Story Without an End.*

SOME THOUGHTS THAT INTRIGUED ME

QUICKEN ME

Many times when discouraged I turn to the Psalms. This is always a thrilling and encouraging experience. The psalmist said in Psalm 119:37, "Quicken thou me in thy way." Many times he repeats this statement in other psalms. The Old Testament writer, conscious of God's important role in his life, acknowledges that God has quickened him or given him life.

"Thy word hath quickened me," stated the psalmist. "With thy precepts thou hast quickened me." Yes, it is when we read the Word that we discover how dead we really are. It is through His Word that we have newness of life. Many times I have been blessed through the words of the Psalms. If this is a good prayer for the Old Testament writer, surely it is a good prayer for you and for me. "Quicken thou me in thy way."

There are times when our spirits are broken, when we cannot get a grip on the promises of God, a time when our faith needs new vitality, and then we need to pray, "Quicken thou me."

I am often amazed at how earnest the men of the world are in their quest for personal gain. Men in business and science put to shame the followers of Jesus Christ when it comes to zeal. Men of the world are zealous, but it seems that Jesus has some lukewarm followers who are more likely to sleep at Gethsemane than to watch with Him one

148

hour.,

The Scripture also admonishes us to be diligent in business. This is one verse that most people in business adhere to very well. But the verse continues, "Fervent in spirit; serving the Lord." Surely with the psalmist we should pray, "Quicken us, O Lord, in thy way, make us fervent in spirit; serving the Lord." Spiritual renewal comes from God. The verse says nothing as to the means by which the Lord is going to use us to quicken other individuals. The psalmist leaves this to God's discretion. I pray that God will always give me the grace to want the "quickening" done in God's way.

DOING WHAT WE CAN

Many years ago I read a poem; three lines of it have meant much to me but I have never found out who really wrote them.

Had I a thousand tongues not one would silent be,

Had I a thousand hearts, dear Lord,

I'd give them all to Thee.

Now I do not have a thousand tongues, nor do I have a thousand hearts, but it is my desire to offer the one I have to the Lord. How ridiculous it is for anyone to offer to God what he does not possess when there is reluctance to dedicate to Him those things we already have.

How simple it is to offer to the Lord the things we do not have. Frankly, I have not been as faithful as I ought to have been with my one tongue and one heart, nor have I always fully dedicated even this one heart and one tongue to the Lord.

This lesson was taught to me through an incident that occurred in 1926. I was listening to the Rev. John Van Ess, a missionary from Arabia. Deeply impressed by the message and the missionary, I promised God, "When this man comes back on his next furlough, I will do something really substantial for his work." You see, I figured that I couldn't give him a substantial gift right then, but perhaps when my business prospered more fully I would be able to give generously. That is where the mistake was made. I was not willing to commit to God what I had that morning.

In 1933, seven years later, I sat in my customary place in the home church and was rather surprised when I noticed Mr. Van Ess sitting in the chair in back of the pulpit. It was then that the promise made seven years before flashed through my mind. However, during the year 1929 the depression had come upon us. Banks had failed. People were unable to pay their mortgages. Homes were foreclosed. The financial situation was very bad. I had been in a better financial position seven years prior to this. If only I had done for God then what I had planned to do later.

Chancellor Adenauer is said to have made a statement that is applicable: "It seems God has put a limit on the wisdom of man, but no limit on his stupidity." We can fool our fellow man with pious statements and promises and commitments of good intent, but we can never fool God.

Keep your promise to God now, do not wait for a more opportune time - it may never come.

A MOST VALUABLE POSSESSION

Redeeming the time is as important a lesson as one can ever learn in life. It is most important that we use our time to the very best of our ability. Time is one of our most valuable possessions, but it is often foolishly squandered. In Ephesians 5:16 we read, "Redeeming the time, because the days are evil." It is evident that unless each one of us learns to redeem the time, the great masses of humanity will never be reached for Christ. It is well to remember constantly that souls are dying every minute and millions are traveling on a road that will lead them to a Christless eternity.

I became acutely aware of this truth recently when I visited the Grand Canyon. Standing on its edge, I recalled that forty years had passed since I had stood in that very place. The words of the psalmist came to my mind, "Teach us to number our days, that we may apply our hearts unto wisdom."

In numbering my days it occurred to me at that time that if I should live threescore years and ten, which is the allotted time, only 2,221 days were left me; now a great number of those days were gone. This might sound rather ridiculous, but I believe that it is well for all of us always to be conscious of the fact that our days are numbered. A friend of mine has a wooden plaque on his desk. There are only two lines, but they certainly express my feelings.

Only one life, 'twill soon be past.

Only what's done for Christ will last!

It is my concern that the days, weeks, months, or years still allotted to me may be used in the service of Christ.

"See then that ye walk circumspectly, not as fools, but as wise, Redeeming the time, because the days are evil." (Ephesians 5:15-16)

PUTTING THE SAINTS IN CIRCULATION

It is said that during the time Alexander the Great was in power a scarcity of silver developed. Alexander sent his scouts throughout the empire to ascertain what silver might be available. When the report was returned, it indicated that the only measurable quantity of available silver was in the form of statues of the gods located in the great temples of the empire. Alexander the Great ordered his soldiers to bring in the statues and melt them down. "Put the saints in circulation," he ordered.

It might not be a bad idea today if all of us were melted

by the fire of the Holy Spirit and molded so that we, too, could be put into circulation. This would be a mighty effective way in which to reach our generation, and to present to them the claims of our Lord Jesus Christ.

LAUNCHING OUT FOR GOD

If you have been praying for years without any evident results, you may be tempted to say with Peter, "Master, we have toiled all night, and have taken nothing." A much more pleasing statement to God, I am sure, would be, "Nevertheless at thy word I will let down the net."

To those of us who do not possess much talent and hardly know how to put what talent we do have to use, it is well to remember that Satan will discourage us from trying again. Jesus told us to sow beside all waters. Many times during the history of the World Home Bible League we have been discouraged, but we have found it rewarding to turn for encouragement to the Scripture we distribute.

Simon Peter's boat full of fish was his reward for launching out at Christ's command. May God also give us the faith to launch out for Him. May we redeem the time He has given us. Then we, too, will receive our just reward.

UNREDEEMED

Have you ever looked into a pawnbroker's window? My, how interesting it is! What a wide assortment of articles: guns, watches, and jewelry of all kinds can be found there! There is a diamond ring; maybe it represents a broken engagement. There is a medal, perhaps won for personal valor on the field of battle. Oh, what stories could be told if every article in the pawnbroker's window could talk.

I was looking in such a window one day and became very interested in the various articles. Over one group was a sign that read "Unredeemed." It brought a smile to my face at first but then my heart began to fill with a strange

152

emotion. The various articles in the window represented treasures of the past, relics of another day, probably a day of great prosperity. What heartaches must have been experienced when they were given in pawn. Probably everyone who deposited an article with the pawnbroker felt that some day it would be redeemed. I glanced at the pawnbroker, who could be seen inside his place of business. He did not seem sentimental at all. It was a cold business proposition and those who had lost the merchandise had paid a just penalty for not having met the demands of their contracts.

What a deadly parallel there is between these articles in the pawnshop window and unregenerate mankind: the high, the low, the strong, the weak, one helpless huddle of humanity. Above them also is written the fateful sign "Unredeemed." There is but one solution, they must be redeemed from sin and returned to their original owner, God, if they are ever to know eternal life. Satan is the unsentimental pawnbroker of lives. He deals harshly. Many trust their lives to his care, feeling there will be time enough to redeem them, but what mortal can meet his full demands. As we look at the lives of men, women, and children who are in the hands of this master pawnbroker we see the sign above them, "unredeemed," and we realize there is only one who has the ability to pay for the broken lives. Jesus Christ did so on Calvary.

The prime objective of Scripture distribution is to introduce Jesus Christ who is willing to stamp "redeemed" upon the lives of lost men and women.

A NECESSARY INGREDIENT

We are certain that the enemies of the gospel of Jesus Christ do not have the answers to life's problems. However, one thing they do not lack is zeal in this great battle for the souls, the minds, and the hearts of men.

153

In Psalm 145:4 we read, "One generation shall praise thy works to another, and shall declare thy mighty acts." Unless we become more effective in sharing the gospel that has been committed to our trust, it will be said of us that which we read in Judges 2:10, "...and there arose another generation after them, which knew not the Lord..."

Prayer is the foundation upon which the World Home Bible League's ministry is built. May God grant that the power of prayer may continue to be evidenced throughout our entire ministry.

God is always faithful in answering our prayers. Therefore, this should encourage us to pray more. The thief on the cross prayed that he might be remembered when our Lord entered into His kingdom, and he too was given more than he asked for; he was given eternal life.

THE URGENT NEED

One day a railroad received delivery of a massive steam engine. On a day appointed it was decided to have a trial run. Officers of the company, from the president down, and the major stockholders were invited to be present. All was in readiness. Promptly at 10 o'clock the president of the railroad mounted the steel steps leading to the cab, raised his hand and pulled out the throttle. There was a hiss of steam but the engine did not move. It was an embarrassing situation.

Immediately there was a considerable amount of discussion among the officers of the company and the stockholders. Finally, one of the vice presidents who had secret aspirations of some day becoming president, boldly spoke up. He said, "I am sure the reason why this engine doesn't move is because it has not been properly oiled and greased." Immediately a crew was summoned. Carefully they aimed their oil at vital places and the engine was thoroughly lubricated.

154

Once again the president mounted the steps, gave a wave of the hand and once more pulled the throttle. Again it hissed but refused to move. At this point one of the stockholders spoke up, "I'm sure that the trouble is not with the engine but with the so-called engineer. What does the president of the outfit know about running a locomotive? What we need is a man especially trained for the job." So they obtained the services of a new engineer. Before he climbed aboard he ordered a crew of men to polish all the brass fittings. Now the brass shone in the sun, the bearings were oiled, the grease cups were filled; surely the problem was solved. Slowly and confidently he pulled out the throttle, but the engine stood still.

Near the track stood an old gray-haired man. A pair of well-worn and improperly fitting overalls draped over his bent figure. He wiped his forehead with an old red handkerchief, walked over to the company managers and said, "I am just an old-timer, but I can guarantee you I know what's wrong. There just isn't a hot enough fire in the boiler!"

We have discovered throughout the many years of the League's existence that the excuses given as to why churches are not going places are varied. Some blame it on the church itself, others say it's the preacher's fault. All types of corrective measures are taken. Although the church should move and be powerful it still lacks something. Some say it's poor organization, others have gone as far as they can to make the church more attractive. They polish the pulpit and furniture, and clean the pews; they obtain the services of a congenial man who is willing to shake hands and go along with the crowd, but the mighty powerful mechanism fails to respond. Oftentimes there is only a hiss of steam and little indication of achievement.

155

What is the answer? The only answer is that there is not a hot enough fire in the boiler. Today there is a growing need for a new anointing by the Holy Spirit that would set afire both the hearts of the men and women in the pew and the heart of the pastor in the pulpit. Then, and only then, can the church move in its God-ordained mission throughout the world.

And how do we get the Holy Spirit? Simply by asking for it. Jesus said, "If ye then, being evil, know how to give good gifts unto your children, how much more shall your Father which is in heaven give good things to them that ask Him?"

TALKING ABOUT EXCUSES

During the many years of the World Home Bible League's existence, its representatives have presented the challenge of Bibleless homes to many communities throughout the nation. Pastors and individual Christians, recognizing their duty, have accepted the challenge and have gone forth from door to door. Hundreds of thousands of people have been invited to church and Sunday school, and Bibles have been placed in Bibleless homes wherever there was a promise that the Scripture would be read.

In bringing this challenge to churches we have often been greatly inspired by the reaction of God's people to their duties. How encouraging it is to see church and pastor work together in an attempt to canvass a community for Christ. But, in this task, we have also heard a multitude of excuses. In fact, one day I made the statement that if there is any subject in the world on which I am an authority it is excuses that people give to avoid Christian service.

Many Christians seem to have hearts as big as the great outdoors, but they are as cold as the bleakest winter day. Other Christians have no time. Still others are much too

156

nervous. Some claim that they are not capable. Others admit they are too scared. A portion of them say they are not good enough for Christian service.

I am reminded of God's encounter with Moses. Moses was trained in the courts of Pharaoh, but when God asked him to go on a mission for Him, Moses had excuse after excuse. "I am not eloquent," he said, and finally after God listened to all of Moses' complaints, Moses lost the opportunity. Aaron, his uneducated brother, was given the privilege of being God's messenger.

It is well to ring the church bells on Sunday morning and let the whole community know that church service is being held, but perhaps it is more important to ring the doorbells throughout the community and invite the people in. "Go out into the highways and hedges, and compel them to come in." The apostle Paul, the greatest missionary who ever lived, did not feel it beneath his dignity to go from house to house, and the victory of the early church was in many ways directly associated with the verse of Scripture that says, "And daily in the temple, and in every house, they ceased not to teach and preach Jesus Christ."

When we hear excuses of men and women we recall an incident that happened many years ago. It involved a crumpled mass of airplane wreckage on the top of Mt. Moran in Wyoming. The plane was owned by a well-known missionary agency. A missionary mother who had boarded the plane said to a bystander as she led her fifth child aboard the aircraft, "Here is the fifth reason that people give me why I should not go to the mission field," but she went anyway.

This missionary mother did not lack excuses. She had the best of them. Only a few months before her husband had met death as a result of a crash in the jungle of a foreign nation. Now there were five little mouths to feed, five little bodies to clothe, and five children to bring up in a cruel world. She could have used every one of those excuses and many more. However, she was resolved that nothing ·would keep her from Christian service. In complete surrender she forgot all the excuses as she pressed toward the goal of her high calling.

In God's indisputable wisdom He took her and the five children in a split moment of terror as the plane struck the mountain top and all were killed

Fellow Christian, what is your excuse? Or have you risen above excuse making? Let us pray that all of us may be obedient to the clearly revealed will of God.

THE TRUE SAYINGS OF GOD

As the League grew older the climate in many churches seemed to change. During the early years only the rankly liberal churches denied the complete authority of the Word. In many ways, it seems that as man becomes more scientifically oriented and mature the more apparent is the increased criticism of the Bible and of its inspiration. It was necessary for the League to take a definite stand and to be more vocal in its position on this matter. As founder of the League, I have always considered an editorial that appeared in the *Sower* some time ago to be our best answer to these attacks. This is the editorial as it appeared in the League's publication, the *Sower*.

Those of us who represent the World Home Bible League do not claim to be great theologians - we are not.

However, we are becoming more and more concerned over the flippant attitude towards God's Word and the malignant teachings that originate at seminary lecterns only to spread to many church pulpits.

We are not attacking the "God is dead" theology; no, the red rose, the blinking star, and the towering mountains dissipate that theory as thoroughly as the bright morning sun dissipates the clinging ground fog. The intense awareness within our own souls of the very presence of God the Father testifies eloquently to us that He lives!

But now there seems to be a more insidious attack upon the very bulwark of our historic Christian faith. We refer to those "intellectual giants" who are constantly at work attempting to pulverize the anvil of God's Word with their puny hammers of human reasoning and intellectual appraisal.

Although some may brand us as incurably naive, it seems to us that Jesus Christ, almost 2,000 years ago, prophetically attacked their modernistic philosophies when He admonished, "Verily I say unto you, Whosoever shall not receive the kingdom of God as a little child, he shall not enter therein." This should have settled for all time, we believe, that faith in God's Word was never intended to be rationalized by man's mind, no matter how highly it may have been trained nor how much of earth's knowledge it may have accumulated.

Some are quick to attack the historicity of the Pentateuch. They limit the intelligence and the ability of God and Creator. Pointing to their achievements they conclude that science has enabled man to escape the law of gravity in capsules that orbit the earth, to walk on the moon, and to cast his eyes on Mars.

All these, they proudly boast, are their attainments, but they refuse to ascribe to God the ability to part the waters of the Sea of Reeds. The stories of Moses and the flight from Egypt are tainted with Jewish folklore, they say, and some of the boldest critics brand them as outright fables. The New Testament miracles are also denied. The cardinal doctrines presented in the Bible are openly mocked. The Scripture's strict moral law is abdicated and replaced by the new morality.

By what conceivable right does finite man question the wisdom and the understanding and ability of an infinite God? Isaiah, that great prophet of the Old Testament, cried, "Hast thou not known? has thou not heard, that the everlasting God, the Lord, the Creator of the ends of the earth, fainteth not, neither is weary? there is no searching of his understanding." (40:28). And, in Ecclesiastes 11:5, still another Old Testament writer asks, "As thou knowest not what is the way of the spirit, nor how the bones do grow in the womb of her that is with child: even so thou knoweth not the works of God who maketh all."

CONFORMITY TO THE WORLD

I read a book on missions which stated, "They don't kill Christians nowadays." It emphasized the fact that today Christians in general live in conformity with the world. Most Christians are no threat to Satan's empire. Unless we become what the early church was, we will not be attacked by Satan. A certain man who knew his own heart well observed, "When it comes to being a witness for my Lord, I feel that I have been 98 percent a coward and if my name was to be written anywhere, it would be worthy only to be written on the yellow pages."

LIFE IS A BATTLE

One day I was to address a group of Christian businessmen in the Republic Building in Chicago. I had come a long distance from a previous meeting, but I arrived on time - in fact, a few minutes early - and was ushered into an adjoining lounge. There was a gentleman sitting in that lounge and we greeted each other. Being very tired, I sat down and remarked, "Life is a battle, isn't it?"

He asked, "Are you a Christian, sir?"

I replied, "Yes, I am a Christian."

He stated, "I'm amazed that you should speak of the Christian life as a battle."

I asked, "Don't you think it is?"

He answered, "Not at all."

I inquired, "Are you going to be in the meeting after a while?"

He said, "Yes."

"Well, I happen to be your speaker and, frankly, I'm too tired to talk to you now but will take care of you later."

After being introduced, I launched into my message: "Gentlemen, life is a battle. Christian living is warfare. If there is anyone within the sound of my voice who doesn't find this business of being the salt, light and witness that the Lord would have us be to be warfare, the chances are that he has never entered into the battle for Christ and His church. If this isn't warfare, why did the apostle Paul say, 'Put on the whole armor of God?' Why did the song writer write, 'Soldiers of Christ, arise' if this isn't warfare? You know where our trouble lies? I am thinking of the little boy who was asked by his Sunday school teacher, 'Is your daddy a Christian?' He said, 'I think he is but he isn't working at it lately.' "

There are people who call themselves Christians but who are not working at it. We have all heard people say, "We're behind the program of the church, we'll back up our pastor and our missionaries. We'll back up the work of the World Home Bible League." Yes, they are behind many things, but when we analyze closely we find that many who speak freely about being behind a program, are

161

so far behind they are not doing any good. We need to enter into this battle, that our lives may be lived in line with the purpose of our existence which is to glorify God. That is what we are here for. That is why we were created. That is why we must carry out the battle of the Lord.

A DEDICATED MINORITY

If we really mean business for God a dedicated minority will be raised up in this hour. This minority will march forth under the banner of the cross of Christ and exert an influence on our generation for the Lord and for His church.

With the proper dedication and unity of purpose this minority will make the Communist programs and all other philosophies look sick. The Christian church does have the answer. All we need is a dedicated faith in the weapon that God has given to us for Christian warfare. The weapon is the sword of the Spirit, the Holy Scripture.

J. HUDSON TAYLOR

The Reverend J. Hudson Taylor, founder of the China Inland Mission, one day said, "I cannot believe that God would have told us to trust in His name and have brought us thus far to put us to shame."

God has brought the ministry of the World Home Bible League to new heights. Certainly, God would not have taught us to trust in His name and then put us to shame. He has told us, "He which hath begun a good work in you will perform it until the day of Jesus Christ," and of this we are confident.

AS UNTO THE LORD!

Many times when I meet with men and women who have put their lives into the ministry of the World Home Bible League I rejoice that these people represent a direct evidence of answered prayer. Early in our ministry, because of my sales background, I would attempt to sell.

162

people on putting their lives into the World Home Bible League ministry. Today, I recognize this as an error. Most of these people have fallen by the wayside because no one loves Bill Chapman enough to put his life and heart into this work and to take the discouragements and disappointments thrown into their path. We need dedicated men and women who do this work as unto the Lord. When it is done in that spirit God supplies the encouragement. He is the source of strength and gives great joy in His service.

THE LAYMAN'S RESPONSIBILITY

Somewhere the statement has appeared, "Ninety-nine and a half percent of all the people in our churches are laymen." There can be no debate on this issue. Sometimes, as we all know, laymen can become very critical. Perhaps we ought to look into the mirror. If we represent ninety-nine percent of the church and much of the church is our responsibility, how come there is so much wrong with it? Do you remember the seventy elders in Numbers 11? There were seventy ordained elders, but we are told only two of them were prophesying in the camp. They were Eldad and Medad. Joshua ran to Moses and reported that Eldad and Medad were prophesying in the camp, and asked Moses to forbid them. It is interesting to note what Moses answered. Did he reprimand them? No, Moses exclaimed, "Would God that all the Lord's people were prophets, and that the Lord would put his Spirit upon them!" So, don't let anyone discourage us in carrying out our responsibility as laymen.

MY GREATEST CONCERN

A great many people have come to me from time to time who are interested and concerned about the future. Some express concern over financial matters and business problems, while others have personal and health problems.

Recently one of these individuals asked, "How do things look to you from a long range?" I answered, "Frankly, my concern is not about tomorrow, next week, or next year, but my concern is whether or not I am living my life in line with the purpose of my existence, which is to glorify God. My concern is to acknowledge Him in every phase of life. I firmly believe that if I do that my future will take care of itself.

A RUT OR A GRAVE

What is rut? Someone said it is a grave with both ends open - you can still get out. Often while in a rut we become determined to live on a higher spiritual level. We begin to meditate upon the Word. We are challenged by it. As a result of prayer we have the courage to rise to a higher level. We step out of the rut in which we find ourselves.

But, on this higher ground all the forces of evil seem to be against us and unless at this point we can have the promises of God brought to our remembrance we will be defeated. We must be fortified by a strong prayer life and by the intercessory prayer of others.

PERSISTENCE IN PRAYER

Intercession and its possibilities have yet to be measured. Has anyone ever really tested the limitation and possibilities of prayer? Have you ever noticed Abraham's intercession for Sodom and Gomorrah? This is an illustration of almost universal failure to test prayer to the limit of its possibilities. Abraham received everything he asked for in this prayer. First he asked the Lord to spare the city if there were fifty righteous persons. God said He would. Gradually Abraham came down. Would God spare the city if there were ten righteous? God said He would.

Why didn't Abraham ask if God would spare the city for five or even one righteous person? Perhaps it was because Abraham, who knew that Lot was a child of God, thought surely he could expect Lot to have an influence for righteousness to the extent of half a convert a year for the twenty years he had spent in Sodom. However, we know that Lot had no such influence and subsequently the city of Sodom was destroyed. The Lord did not stop giving; Abraham stopped asking. Let us be persistent in prayer.

WANT TO KNOW MORE?

QUESTIONS AND ANSWERS

A great number of interesting questions have been directed to officers and staff members of the League by people attempting to gain an understanding of the League's ministry.

Some of these questions follow.

1. Isn't there considerable overlapping in the field of Bible distribution with so many agencies doing the same type of work?

All the work done by the Bible-distribution agencies is affecting at the present time only a small percentage of the world's population. The literacy rate, the increased population trends, and even the ecumenical movement, are helping to create a greater demand than ever before for the Printed Page. It is far beyond the ability of all the Bible societies of the world to meet this need adequately.

It should be noted that although all societies engaged in Bible distribution seem to be busy in the same work, they do have different emphases. Some are completely dedicated to Scripture translation, some to Scripture distribution; others believe that the Scripture they make available should be sold; however, some give the Scripture away. Some societies operate only in certain geographical patterns, and others appeal to specific language groups.

166

2. Why couldn't the same work be done by one highly centralized agency?

Although this appears to be a logical suggestion, it is not. One could also ask the question, why aren't all the needs of higher education met by one college? Why should there be different colleges even within one denomination?

For many years the bulk of Scripture distribution was under the complete control of one organization, but is this right? Should any Bible society have complete monopoly of all Scripture translation, distribution, and allocation? A free spirit of Christian competition, we believe, is both helpful and beneficial. The imagination and the enthusiasm of independent groups have greatly multiplied Scripture distribution throughout the world.

3. Does the World Home Bible League cooperate with any other distribution agency?

The World Home Bible League cooperates with such ministries as the New York Bible Society, the Russian Bible Society, the Trinitarian Bible Society, Scripture Gift Mission, and others. The League also works very closely with Bible translators, such as the Lockman Foundation of California, publishers of the *Amplified New Testament* and the *New American Standard Bible,* and with Tyndale House, publishers of *The Living Series*.

The World Home Bible League also counts it a privilege to cooperate with the Wycliffe Bible Translators and is today one of its chief publishers of materials in tribal languages and dialects of Mexico and South America. Such cooperative programs save money. Other programs of sharing Bible and Testament printing plates with other agencies have saved additional revenue.

4. How many missionaries do you employ?

The World Home Bible League is a service organization. It employs no missionaries. We believe it is the duty of the organized church to do this type of work. Independent and denominational missionaries receive Scripture we produce and distribute it throughout the world. A partial list of missionary agencies and denominations distributing World Home Bible League Scripture can be found on pages 179 to 183.

5. How is your ministry supported?

The World Home Bible League does not have a foundation underwriting it nor does it have any reserve funds. We are a faith organization supported principally by the gifts of God's people through individual gifts, offerings in churches, and contributions made by businessmen. On pages 169 to 174 there is supplementary information giving you some idea of how churches, groups, or individuals can help support the World Home Bible League's growing ministry.

These are only a few of the questions that have been asked. Perhaps there are other questions in your mind. Those who wish to learn more about the actual program of the League, its geographical boundaries, its statistical information on distribution, publication, and finance, are encouraged to study the following facts concerning the League.

FAITH IN ACTION PROGRAMS

CHURCH OFFERINGS

The World Home Bible League encourages church offerings. Some churches have placed the League on their budgets and take one or two offerings a year so that the ministry can continue to maintain an effective influence.

SHARE PROGRAM

It is possible for your church or society, or even an individual, to take a share. Shares are available for Wycliffe Bible Translation projects in amounts of $300 to $5,000. Other shares for Scripture distribution programs in given areas can also be had.

CHURCH AND SOCIETY PROGRAMS

The League furnishes speakers, films, or slides and encourages the local church to sponsor a program. The offering received goes for Scripture for the Bibleless homes of the world.

WORLD BANKS

More than 10,000 families across the U.S.A. and Canada have the popular World Home Bible League bank. These families are encouraged to give five cents a day toward Scripture distribution. So far more than one million dollars has come to the League through this source. Why not get in touch with us and have us send you a world bank for your family's use?

CALENDAR

A systematic way of giving a dollar or more a month is

through our calendar program. Thousands of homes have these calendars. Each month is designated for a special mission interest and families are encouraged to pray for a given area. Some families report increased missionary interest.

COIN CARDS

The ideal way to raise money for the purchase of Scripture, Testaments, or Scripture portions, particularly in Sunday school classes, is through the coin card system. The League provides the coin cards. They hold thirty dimes. The coin cards are filled with a particular field in mind, such as Puerto Rico, Mexico, etc. In this way children are encouraged early in life to set aside some money for missions.

GIFTS

Many of our sowers have asked how they can arrange for greater help to the World Home Bible League and still care for their daily needs. These inquirers are keenly aware of the responsibilities of Christian stewardship. We can suggest a few ways.

GIFT ANNUITIES

The donor gives an amount of money to the League and the League, in turn, agrees to pay interest on the amount given during the lifetime of the donor or, if it is a joint gift with another, during the lifetime of the survivor. The annual rate of interest depends on the age of the donor, or donors of a joint gift.

GIFTS BY WILLS

One of the last acts of stewardship for any Christian is making his will. In your will you can provide for an outright bequest to the League of money or property. If there are certain persons for whom you wish to provide an income for a specified time, you can make a testamentary trust and arrange for the income of your property to go to these individuals, with provisions that the property or trust estate be turned over to the League when the requirements have been met.

GIFTS OF REAL ESTATE

Real estate in many instances has appreciated in value and many owners do not want to sell because of taxes. A gift of real estate to the League may be of benefit to the donor.

GIFTS OF STOCKS OR BONDS

Stocks or bonds may be treated in the same way as real estate.

These are but a few suggestions; your attorney can suggest other ways. If you have any questions concerning any of these matters, please write us. Many plans offer real tax savings to you. Our attorneys would gladly work out a plan to fit your particular need.

LIVING MEMORIAL TRIBUTES

It is becoming more and more customary for thoughtful people to express their sympathy by perpetuating a friend or loved one's memory in a way that will benefit the living. Frequently this is a charitable gift either in lieu of flowers, or in addition to a floral tribute. Such contributions from individuals or groups to The World Home Bible League are known as Living Memorial Tributes for they live on in our ministry for Christ around the world.

The World Home Bible League gratefully receives these meaningful expressions of sympathy and promptly sends an appropriate card to the family of the person in whose memory the contribution is given. The donor's name appears on the card; however, the amount of the contribution is not revealed. Gifts of $10 or more will be permanently recorded in the Book of Remembrance which is kept on display at international headquarters, 16801 Van Dam Road, South Holland, Illinois. In addition to the above acknowledgments, all gifts will receive further mention in the League's publication, THE SOWER. Each contributor receives an official acknowledgment for income tax purposes.

QUALIFIED SPEAKERS

Staff members are all convinced of the Holy Spirit's inspiration of the Scripture and are prepared to bring challenging messages on the need of Bible distribution, the importance of community canvasses, and also to give some excellent examples of how the Word of God has changed the lives of men and women.

MISSIONS

The World Home Bible League staff is constantly in touch with missionaries and mission stations throughout the world. If anyone is qualified to speak on the subject of missions and their need in the world today, Bible League personnel are. Directly associated with missionary efforts· in India, Africa, Japan, and elsewhere, our personnel can make a great contribution to any missionary conference.

BIBLE

The need of the Bible in various lands and on the home front is one of the favorite subjects of our deputation staff. Armed with statistics, remarks and reports from many strategic places, staff members of the World Home Bible League have many messages to give on the subject of the Bible, its need in the world today, its power among those who are unsaved, and its effectiveness as a weapon of missionary endeavor.

GREAT MANDATE

The World Home Bible League personnel also believe in the great mandate given by Christ to the church, "Go ye into all the world, and preach the Gospel to every creature." Qualified speakers with messages on this subject are available for your church services.

INSTRUCTION

Some of our personnel are experienced in setting up local and regional canvasses, and are available to give instructions to your workers. The League has sponsored canvasses in·such areas as Redlands, California; Phoenix, Arizona; Grand Rapids, Michigan; and such sizable programs as Scripture distribution for the entire San Diego County, and Scripture distribution in every Negro home in the state of Mississippi.

FILMS

The World Home Bible League maintains a library of motion picture films and slide programs. These films depict the work in many countries. Motion picture films on Bible subjects are also available.

THE WORLD HOME BIBLE LEAGUE — WHAT IT IS

The World Home Bible League is an interdenominational and an international organization. Our prime objective is the distribution of the Bible or a portion of it to every Bibleless home in the world. As a service organization we are dedicated to the task of providing the Scripture in the languages of the people through the organized church, its pastors, missionaries, and lay workers.

Although the World Home Bible League is committed to a general policy of free Scripture distribution, there are times when, upon a missionary's advice, a small token charge is accepted from those who receive our material. We insist, however, that no one shall be denied the privilege of owning a copy of the Bible due to lack of finances on his part.

The following three rules govern our free Bible distribution:

1. There should be no other Bible in the home.
2. There should be a promise made that it will be read.
3. Wherever possible, the Scripture must be placed by a representative of the church.

OUR PUBLICATION — THE SOWER

Approximately ten times a year we publish a magazine called, "The Sower." This is circulated to all those who are interested in our ministry. The Sower, edited by Mr. William Ackerman and Mrs. Marian Injerd, enjoys a very good reception.

The Sower contains interesting developments in the work, new projections, new publications, and news in general concerning Bible Distribution in the U.S.A., Canada, and overseas.

The Sower is sent to you free of charge. If you would like to be placed on the mailing list, please refer to the postcard enclosed in the back of this book.

COOPERATING CHURCHES AND DENOMINATIONS

The distribution of Scripture through the World Home Bible League is on an interdenominational basis. We are grateful that evangelical churches within many denominations continue to support the League through their offerings. Among them are the following:

Apostolic Christian
Assembly of God
Bible
Brethren
Brethren-Evangelical United
Christian
Christian and Missionary Alliance
Christian Reformed
Church of Christ
Church of God
Community
Congregational
Conservative Baptist
Covenant Church of America
Episcopal
Evangelical Free
Four Square
Free Will Baptist
Full Gospel
General Association Regular Baptist
Independent Fundamental Churches of America

Lutheran
Methodist
Moody Memorial and other independent churches
Nazarene
Orthodox Presbyterian
Pilgrim Holiness
Reformed Church of America
Salvation Army
Southern Baptist Convention
United Presbyterian

MISSIONS

The Bible still remains the Sword of the Spirit. Recognizing this, missions in our homeland use the Bible extensively in the hope of converting the unsaved. Scripture furnished by us has gone to rescue missions, family missions, and missions to ethnic groups. A partial list follows:

American Soul Clinic
Arbuckel Shelter House, Greenfield, Illinois
Bible Missionary Association, Hubbard Lake, Michigan
Bible Rescue Mission, Chicago, Illinois
Border Missions, Hidalgo, Texas
Brainerd Indian Missions, Hot Springs, South Dakota
Buffalo Hebrew Christian Mission, Syracuse, New York
Calvary Wayside Chapel, Pella, Iowa
Campus Crusade for Christ
Caravan Program - Reformed Churches
Chapel Crusaders Mission, South Bay, Florida
Child Evangelism Fellowship
Christian Salvage Mission, Howell, Michigan
City Gospel Mission, Cincinnati, Ohio
City Rescue Mission, San Diego, California
Cuban Mission, Key West, Florida
Evangelical Wesleyan Mission, Key West, Florida
Faith Missions, Yuma, Arizona
Glad Tidings Mission, Chicago, Illinois
Golden Faith Mission, Columbia, South Carolina

Good Samaritan Mission, Inc., Selma, California
Gospel Fellowship Mission, Greenville, South Carolina
Helping Hand Rescue Mission, Huntington Station,
    New York
Holland City Missions, Holland, Michigan
Home Ministry Fellowship, Spring Valley, California
Indian Mission, Farmington, New Mexico and Rosebud,
    South Dakota
International Mission Foundation, Pasadena, California
Jewish Christian Shalom Center, San Francisco,
    California
Jollet Bible Mission, Elkton, Virginia
Kentucky Mountain Mission, Beattyville, Kentucky
Latin Home Missionary Association, San Benito, Texas
    and Tiffin, Ohio
Mexican Gospel Mission, Inc., Phoenix, Arizona
Mid-America Mission, Inc., Green Forest, Arkansas
Ministry to Seamen, New Orleans, Louisiana
Missionary and Soul Winning Fellowship, San Ysidro,
    California
National Child Salvation, Brooklyn, New York
National Home Missions Fellowship, Cucumber,
    West Virginia
Needy Soul's Mission, Inc., Imperial Beach, California
Pacific Garden Mission (Unshackled), Chicago, Illinois
Pan American Literature Mission, Inc., Tucson, Arizona
Rehoboth Mission, Rehoboth, New Mexico
Rock Bottom Evangelistic Association, Turlock,
    California
Rockford Rescue Mission, Rockford, Illinois
Seamen's Mission, Chicago, Illinois
South Arizona and Sonora Mexico Mission, Inc., Tucson,
    Arizona
South Side Union Chapel, Olean, New York

Spanish Baptist Mission, Paterson, New Jersey
Sunshine Mission, St. Louis, Missouri
Swedish Free Mission, Tucson, Arizona
S.W.I.M. Program of the Christian Reformed Church
Tecate Mission, Tecate, California
Teen Challenge Training Center, Rehrersburg,
    Pennsylvania
The Mel Trotter Mission, Grand Rapids, Michigan
The Star of Hope, El Monte, California
Utah Bible Mission, Inc., Salt Lake City, Utah
Valley Missions, Fresno, California
Village Missions, Two Buttes, Colorado
West Side Rescue Mission, Chicago, Illinois

EDUCATIONAL INSTITUTIONS

The Bible is not permitted to be read in most schools today. Many teachers, however, feel that there are opportunities to place Scriptures in the hands of many pupils. In some areas, Bibles and Testaments are requested for release time classes. Bible schools, seminaries, etc., use World Home Bible League Scriptures in their practical work assignments, Shipments of Bibles, Testaments, and portions have been sent for distribution to the following:

American Christian School, Norfolk, Virginia
Appalachian Bible Institute, Bradley, West Virginia
Azusa Pacific College, Azusa, California
Berean Bible College, Calgary, Alberta, Canada
Bethania Seminary, Guam
Bethany Bible College, Santa Cruz, California
Bethel Bible School, Signal Mountain, Tennessee
Bible Institute of New England, St. Johnsbury, Vermont
Board of Education, Zeeland, Michigan
Bryan College, Dayton, Tennessee
Calvin College, Grand Rapids, Michigan
Carleton College, Northfield, Minnesota
Chicago Christian High School, Palos Heights, Illinois
Chicago Southwest Christian School, Oak Lawn, Illinois
Christian Counseling and Education Center, Short Hills, New Jersey
Clearwater Christian College, Clearwater, Florida
Concordia Senior College, Ft. Wayne, Indiana

Delta State College, Cleveland, Mississippi
Denver Christian Schools, Denver, Colorado
Elim Bible Institute, Lima, New York
Elohim Bible Institute, Castile, New York
Emory University, Atlanta, Georgia
Faith Christian School, Overland, Missouri
Florida Bible College, Miami, Florida
Garden Grove Christian School, Garden Grove,
    California
Gatesville State School for Boys, Gatesville, Texas
Georgia Bible Institute, Athens, Georgia
Glenwood School for Boys, Glenwood, Illinois
Gordon Divinity School, Wenham, Massachusetts
Government Training College, Ghana
Grace Theological Seminary, Warsaw, Indiana
Holiness Bible School, Gravette, Arkansas
Holland High School, Holland, Michigan
Holland Senior High School, Holland, Michigan
Hudsonville Christian School, Hudsonville, Michigan
Immanuel Christian School, Randolph, Wisconsin
Iowa State University, Ames, Iowa
Juan Calvino Seminary, Mexico City, Mexico
Lansing Christian School, Lansing, Illinois
Latin American Bible Institute, La Puente, California
Maranatha Bible Institute, Brazil
Miramonte School, Mountain View, California
Moody Bible Institute, Chicago, Illinois
New Tribes Institute, Jersey Shore, Pennsylvania
Overland Christian Grade School, Overland, Missouri
Pillsbury College, Owatonna, Minnesota
Pine Mountain Settlement School, Pine Mountain
    Kentucky
Redlands Release-Time Bible School, Oregon City,
    Oregon

Reformed Bible Institute, Grand Rapids, Michigan
South Carolina School for Girls, Columbia,
    South Carolina
Southern Normal High School, Brewton, Alabama
Southwestern Bible College, Birmingham, Alabama
Ten Mile School, Ten Mile, Tennessee
Trinity Christian College, Palos Heights, Illinois
Trinity Lutheran School, Lansing, Illinois
Tuskegee Institute, Tuskegee, Alabama
Vennard College, Cleveland, Mississippi
Western Christian High School, Hull, Iowa
Western Theological Seminary, Holland, Michigan
Westminster Seminary, Chestnut Hill, Pennsylvania
Westminster Theological Seminary, Philadelphia,
    Pennsylvania
West Side Christian School, Grand Rapids, Michigan
Wheaton College, Wheaton, Illinois
Wyoming Public Schools, Grand Rapids, Michigan
Zion Bible Institute, East Providence, Rhode Island

HOSPITALS AND INSTITUTIONS

For many years the Gideons have placed Bibles in hotels and institutions and they are to be highly commended for this. However, there are many special situations where people want a foreign language Bible, a large-print New Testament, or some special Scripture booklet that varies concerning content, etc. Pastors and Christian workers affiliated with churches of many denominations continually ask for this type of material. A representative list of hospitals and institutions in which our Scriptures have been placed follows:

Alamosa Community Hospital, Alamosa, Colorado
Arthur J. Audy Home for Children, Chicago, Illinois
Attala Dental Clinic, Kosciusko, Mississippi
Baton Rouge General Hospital, Baton Rouge, Louisiana
Belmont Hospital, Chicago, Illinois
Bethesda Hospital, Denver, Colorado
Brooklyn State Hospital, Brooklyn, New York
Calvary Rehabilitation Center, Phoenix, Arizona
Cherry Hospital, Goldsboro, North Carolina
Christian Medical College Hospital, Vellore, India
Convalescent Homes, Oak Park, Chicago, Illinois
Cook County Hospital, Chicago, Illinois
Fresno General Hospital, Fresno, California
Holland Home, Chicago, Illinois
Hospital Chaplain's Ministry, Tucson, Arizona
Hospital Visitation Group, Denver, Colorado

Lemon Grove Medical Group, Lemon Grove, California
Mary Lott Lyle Hospital, Madanapalle, India
Manteno State Hospital, Manteno, Illinois
Maple Street Clinic Building, Forest Grove, Oregon
Municipal Tuberculosis Sanitarium, Chicago, Illinois
New Castle State Hospital, New Castle, Indiana
Oak Forest Hospital, Oak Forest, Illinois
Sunshine Hospital, Grand Rapids, Michigan
Tabernacle Healing Temple, Brooklyn, New York
Third Field Hospital, San Francisco, California
Veterans Administration Hospital, Marion, Indiana
Veterans Home of California, Napa County, California
West Tennessee Tuberculosis Hospital, Memphis,
    Tennessee
Willows Nursing Home, Ceres, California

PRISONS

Most people think of home in terms of a cottage or ranch type home in a suburb, or perhaps a farm house, or even an apartment. However, there are many people whose home is a jail cell.

Although there are Scriptures available in prisons, special editions are in constant demand. The World Home Bible League, through the churches, supply these. When a prisoner is released, he is encouraged to take along a copy of the Scripture made available to him. A partial list of prisons where League materials have been distributed follows:

Bradford County Jail, Towanda, Pennsylvania
California Men's Colony-East, Los Padres, California
Chicago House of Correction, Chicago, Illinois
Commonwealth of Pennsylvania: Huntington, Bellefonte,
    Philadelphia, Craterford
Dade County Jail, Miami, Florida
Department of Correction, Grass Lake, Michigan
Department of Correction, Jackson, Michigan
Florida State Prison, Radford, Florida
Indiana State Prison, Michigan City, Indiana
Prison, Association, Phoenix, Arizona
Prison, Gowen, Michigan
Prison, Fort Worth, Texas
Prison, Huntsville, Texas
Prison, Kissimmee, Florida

Prison, Oviedo, Florida
Prison, Port Huron, Michigan
Prison, Wichita, Kansas
South Dakota State Penitentiary, Sioux Falls,
    South Dakota

CHURCHES SUPPLY VOLUNTEER WORKERS

The following churches have helped reduce the cost of Scripture production, thanks to the volunteer workers they have supplied in our Operation Handclasp Program:

Alsip Reformed Church, Alsip, Illinois
Beacon Light Christian Reformed Church, Gary, Indiana
Bellevue Baptist Church, Roseland, Chicago, Illinois
Bethany Christian Reformed Church, South Holland, Illinois
Bethel Christian Reformed Church, Lansing, Illinois
Bethel Reformed Church, Harvey, Illinois
Calvary Reformed Church, South Holland, Illinois
Church of God, Power Tower, Chicago, Illinois
Community Reformed Church, Dolton, Illinois
Cornell Avenue Baptist Church, Chicago, Illinois
Cottage Grove Christian Reformed Church, South Holland, Illinois
De Motte Christian Reformed Church, De Motte, Indiana
De Motte Reformed Church, De Motte, Indiana
Des Plaines Christian Reformed Church, Des Plaines, Illinois
Emmanuel Reformed Church, Roseland, Chicago, Illinois
Faith Reformed Church, South Holland, Illinois
First Baptist Church, East Gary, Indiana

First Baptist Church, South Holland, Illinois
First Christian Reformed Church, Highland, Indiana
First Christian Reformed Church, Lansing, Illinois
First Christian Reformed Church, Oak Lawn, Illinois
First Christian Reformed Church, Roseland, Chicago, Illinois
First Christian Reformed Church, South Holland, Illinois
First Methodist Church, Lansing, Illinois
First Reformed Church, Lansing, Illinois
First Reformed Church, Roseland, Chicago, Illinois
First Reformed Church, South Holland, Illinois
Fourth Christian Reformed Church, Roseland, Chicago, Illinois
Grace Reformed Church, Lansing, Illinois
Hobart Woodale Baptist Church, Hobart, Indiana
Immanuel United Church of Christ, Dolton, Illinois
Ivanhoe Reformed Church, Riverdale, Illinois
Lorimer Baptist Church, Dolton, Illinois
Momence Christian Reformed Church, Momence, Illinois
Munster Christian Reformed Church, Munster, Indiana
Oak Forest Baptist Church, Oak Forest, Illinois
Oak Glen Christian Reformed Church, Lansing, Illinois
Oak Park Christian Reformed Church, Oak Park, Illinois
Palos Heights Christian Reformed Church, Palos Heights, Illinois
Park Lane Christian Reformed Church, Evergreen Park, Illinois
Redeemer Lutheran Church, South Holland, Illinois
Riverside Reformed Church, Hammond, Indiana
Ross Reformed Church, Gary, Indiana
Sauk Village Bible Church, Sauk Village, Illinois
State Street Baptist Church, Hammond, Indiana
Temple Baptist Church, Chicago Heights, Illinois

Trinity Lutheran Church, Lansing, Illinois
Trinity Reformed Church, Munster, Indiana
Twenty-Sixth Street Baptist Church, Berwyn, Illinois
United Presbyterian Church, South Holland, Illinois
Village Evangelical Free Church, South Holland, Illinois
Woodmar Baptist Church, Gary, Indiana

OUR WORLD–WIDE MINISTRY

The World Home Bible League has published Scriptures translated into the following languages and dialects:

Arabic	Korean
Bengali	Malayalam
Bulu	Marathi
Chinese	Norwegian
English	Oriva
Finnish	Polish
French	Portuguese
German	Sahu
Greek	Sinhalese
Gujerati	Spanish
Hausa	Swedish
Hindi	Tamil
Italian	Tiv
Japanese	Urdu
Kanada	

The League has also published tribal language Scriptures translated by the Wycliffe Bible Translators in the following countries:

Country	Dialects
Bolivia	8
Brazil	6
India	1
Mexico	39
New Guinea	18

North American Branch	5
Peru	34
Philippines	2
Colombia	1
Vietnam	1

League Scripture has been sent to the following countries:

Australia	Jordan
Argentina	Kenya
Bahamas	Korea
Belgium	Kuwait
Biafra	Lebanon
Bolivia	Liberia
Brazil	Malaysia
Cameroons	Mexico
Canada	Netherlands
Canary Islands	New Zealand
Ceylon	Nigeria
Chile	Persian Gulf States
Colombia	Peru
Congo	Philippines
Costa Rica	Portugal
Denmark	Puerto Rico
Dominican Republic	Republic of South Africa
Ecuador	Sierra Leone
Fiji	Singapore
Ghana	Spain
Gold Coast	Tanganyika
Honduras	Tanzania
Hong Kong	Togo
Indonesia	Uruguay
Italy	U.S.S.R.
Ivory Coast	Vietnam
Jamaica	West Indies
Japan	Zambia

BOARD MEMBERS - 1970

Mr. William A. Chapman, Founder
Mr. Chester L. Evers, Sr., Chairman of the Board
Mr. Herman A. Chapman, President
Mr. Ben Ottenhoff, Vice President
Mr. Fred Post, Secretary
Mr. Stuart De Jong, Treasurer
Mr. Henry Verbeek, Asst. Treasurer
Mr. Evert Cooper
Mr. John Van Ramshorst
Mr. Paul Baker
Col. Henry J. Ramaker
Mr. Robert A. Laning
Mr. Maurice Paterik
Mr. Anthony Van Den Berg
Mr. Lawrence J. Postmus
Mr. Edward Tanis
Mr. William Kuiper, Sr.
Mr. John Rosier
Mr. Robert Billstrand
Mr. Tunis Miedema
Mr. Martin Ozinga, Jr.
Mr. Clarence Smit
Mr. Chester Evers, Jr.
Mr. William J. Huizenga
Mr. William Ackerman, International Director
Mrs. Marian Injerd, Assistant to the Director

REPRESENTATIVES
Mr. Anthony Klingenberg
Mr. William Brondyk
Mr. Derwin Hesselink
Mr. Jacob Porter
Mr. Roy Elsenbroek
Rev. Cecil Staton
Rev. John Van Harn, Church Relations Director,
    Reformed Church in America
BIBLE STUDIES
Rev. John De Vries
WOMEN'S DIVISION
Mrs. John Van Harn
CANADIAN HOME BIBLE LEAGUE
Mr. John Vander Boom, Director
Representatives:
    Rev. Fred Tiessen
    Mr. L. Vanden Top
    Mr. W. Groen
Representatives in many other areas of the world.
SCRIPTURES UNLIMITED BOARD
World Home Bible League:
    Herman Chapman, President
    William Ackerman
    C. L. Evers, Sr., Treasurer
    Ben Ottenhoff
New York Bible Society:
    Rev. Y. R. Kindberg
    John J. Kubach, Vice-president
    James W. Straub, Secretary
    Robert F. Nelson